Management Practice
and Mispractice

The task of management has become increasingly complex in recent years. Chief executives and senior management are confronted with the task of making sense of the multiple factors affecting business systems, and identifying causal relationships in seemingly unstructured problems.

In the field of management a wide gulf exists between theory and practice. Pronouncements from theorists have become increasingly unintelligible to practitioners. Practical propositions from management consultants – often in the form of recipes derived from experience and case studies – are often based on limited hard evidence. This has given rise to many fashions in management. The danger of fashionable doctrines is that they can lead to the adoption of what may be regarded as *management mispractices*, namely practices based on questionable beliefs and premises.

Management Practice and Mispractice is written for managers, management consultants and students of management. The topics and problems discussed will provoke the reader to think about the many issues involved and to question the established doctrines and beliefs.

Professor Samuel Eilon was formerly head of the Management Faculty at Imperial College (London) and is now Emeritus Professor of the University of London and a member of the Monopolies and Mergers Commission in the UK.

Management
Practice
and
Mispractice

SAMUEL EILON

London and New York

First published 1992
by Routledge
11 New Fetter Lane, London EC4P 4EE

Simultaneously published in the USA and Canada
by Routledge
a division of Routledge, Chapman and Hall, Inc.
29 West 35th Street, New York, NY 10001

Typeset in 11 on 13 point Garamond by
Nene Phototypesetters Ltd, Northampton
Printed and bound in Great Britain by
Mackays of Chatham PLC, Chatham, Kent

*British Library Cataloguing in Publication Data
is available on request*

ISBN 0-415-07598-X

*Library of Congress Cataloging in Publication Data
is available on request*

ISBN 0-415-07598-X

To:

Amir
Ronit
Carmel
Daniel

Contents

Preface   xi

1 Structuring the unstructured   1
2 Mission incomplete   15
3 Determinants of corporate performance   25
4 Board size and corporate failure   39
5 OR at the top?   48
6 A simple formula   60
7 The bottom-liners   71
8 A misleading performance measure   83
9 Prominent performance ratios   89
10 Use and misuse of productivity ratios   105
11 A cake can be cut in many ways   114
12 A transfer pricing saga   125
13 Divide and rule   134
14 Management performance appraisal   149
15 What makes Sammy run?   162
16 Don't spit in the soup, we all have to eat   181
17 The role of business schools   190
18 Business policy for beginners   200

Index   211

Preface

Evaluation of performance of business enterprises tends to intensify with the publication of their annual and semi-annual reports, followed by commentaries from stockbrokers and analysts published in the financial press. Captains of industry may not have to suffer the indignity of almost weekly public opinion polls that constantly plague politicians, but views expressed by analysts, and those canvassed among customers, shareholders and investors, serve as powerful reminders to senior executives that the business world is subject to many upheavals and that even the most seemingly secure can suddenly fall from grace.

This vulnerability is put into sharp focus by the stick and carrot syndrome, which is very much in evidence both in business and industry. Successful enterprises with good ratings are offered almost limitless credit at very attractive terms, and their shares are highly valued and provide, not only excellent security for borrowings, but constitute an effective paper currency for expansion and take-overs. At the same time, senior executives of successful enterprises enjoy fabulous remuneration packages, including many non-monetary incentives, and they are constantly sought after in business and social circles. In contrast, poor corporate performance leads to a credit squeeze and mounting pressure on the management from banks, shareholders and would-be investors. *Coups d'états* in boardrooms, hostile take-overs and wholesale reorganizations, all of which often result in job losses at all levels of the managerial hierarchy, even at the very top, are sufficiently common to make executives extremely nervous about the future.

There is, therefore, much to gain from corporate success and everything to lose from failure, both for the enterprise and for those who lead it. A striking feature of the business scene is that it is dominated by two major considerations: The first is the undue emphasis put by the financial world on the short-term perception of corporate performance (and hence the preoccupation with reported financial results and published commentaries), and the second concerns the great inertia of large business systems and the difficulties encountered in trying to change them. Thus, the CEO (Chief Executive Officer) is faced with the constant dilemma that while his (or her) performance is often judged by the here and now, it takes considerable time for a change in the organization to manifest itself, particularly when changes in strategy are called for, such as strategies concerning the range of products and services, quality and pricing policies, concentration on prime markets, corporate size, policy towards innovation, personnel recruitment and training, and so on.

The obvious question that needs to be asked is: What is meant by 'corporate success'? How is it to be defined, and can it be measured? When questioned on these matters, senior executives tend to cite the following ten attributes of success:

- a happy, well-trained and efficient workforce
- a highly motivated and suitably rewarded managerial hierarchy
- satisfied customers and a strong standing in the market, with an effective distribution system, as evidenced by an improving market share
- secure sources of supply for all material inputs from content and reliable suppliers
- good corporate performance, as judged by an accepted range of financial criteria
- high rating in the stock market and among financial analysts
- loyal shareholders and a high reputation among investors
- immunity from predators and hostile take-overs
- good credit lines at reasonable terms
- being well placed to take advantage of innovation and manage new developments

Many of these attributes of success are interdependent, or are conditional on the attainment of others. This list of desiderata can be dismissed as banal statements reminiscent of slogans proclaiming the virtues of clean living and motherhood. But a closer examination of the industrial scene suggests that, to a greater or lesser extent, senior executives do focus on them, as tangible objectives to aim for, and this gives rise to a number of interesting observations.

xii

First, and perhaps the most important issue that senior executives are concerned with, is how to proceed from initially nebulous ideas about objectives to more structured programmes of action (certain aspects of these problems are discussed in Chapters 1 and 2 of this book), to determine what modes of managerial style and control enhance the probability or certainty of success (Chapters 3 and 4), and to consider various organizational formats that can contribute to that end (Chapters 5 and 13). And since ultimately it is through people that success is brought about, it is necessary to ponder on ways in which individual performance can be evaluated and adequately compensated (Chapters 14 and 15).

Secondly, not all industrialists see the objectives listed earlier as equally important. Their ranking does not depend just on the industrial sector to which their enterprise belongs, or to the position held by the enterprise within that sector, but also on many other factors: the history of the organization, the dynamics of the market-place and the strength of the competitors, the threats and opportunities envisaged for the whole sector in general and for the enterprise in particular, and perhaps above all on the personality, ethos and aspirations of the man (or woman) at the top. Some senior executives may dismiss particular objectives as being of minor consequence, while singling out others for special attention. The formulation of objectives and the preoccupation with short-term performance can have far-reaching consequences for the enterprise (as discussed in Chapters 6 and 7).

Thirdly, as any manager faced with multi-criteria knows only too well, corporate objectives are not always compatible with each other, and many may be found to be in direct conflict (these issues and the choice of measurement criteria are debated in Chapters 8 and 9). Even when senior executives are prepared to rank objectives – an exercise that many are loath to perform – the result cannot provide relative weights and trade-offs between objectives in a form that can be converted into an all-embracing single objective function. Furthermore, whatever ranking is produced may well alter with time, depending on changing external and internal circumstances, so that objectives often become moving and fuzzy targets. Also, each of the objectives is itself an amalgam of many more specific attributes and criteria. For example, when managers concentrate on financial performance they soon discover that this involves a host of financial characteristics and ratios, and these too may be compatible or incompatible with each other (Chapters 8 and 9).

The wide range of possible performance criteria raises serious questions of definition and measurement. One example in that area is the manner in which costs are determined, and it is not difficult to demonstrate the profound effect that basic concepts and conventions can have on the results (as shown in Chapters 11 and 12). Another example is the popular area of productivity analysis, which begs the question of what productivity means and how it can be measured (this is discussed in Chapter 10).

All these issues are intertwined and cannot be considered in isolation and this is what makes any coherent and methodical discussion of the management task so difficult. There is no obvious starting set of premises on which a complete theory of management can be systematically constructed on the lines of Euclidean geometry. It has been argued that the managerial task can be equated with making decisions, so that analysis of the decision-making process through modelling can provide the insight that students of management are looking for. An allied proposition is that the logical sequence in which elements of the managerial process can be analysed is to start with a definition (or at least a description) of the purpose of an organization, of what is popularly called its 'mission'. Once you know where you are going, you can proceed to determine the route for getting there. This 'ends and means' approach has a natural intuitive appeal and has kept management consultants in business for decades, but converting this approach into reality is fraught with many difficulties (as Chapters 1 and 2 suggest).

The same is true about many other issues that both theorists and practitioners take for granted. The theorists pontificate in obtuse language about paradigms and the prevalence of professional bureaucracy as a manifestation of a formal analysis of assumptions and beliefs. In contrast, there are practitioners who manage by the seat of their pants, who spurn theory and embrace adhocracy. They do not accept the supremacy of methodology or the need for consistency and are content to leave the decision environment entirely fluid. Others among the management consultants' fraternity are convinced that experience gained from tackling a problem in one company can be relevant and useful in handling a new problem in another company, even when it is entirely different in many respects and belongs to a different industrial sector; they firmly believe that accumulated experience can teach managers to discern ways of bringing order and control into decaying business systems that need to be revived.

The result is that a wide gulf now exists between theory and practice. The theorists talk to other theorists, and their pronouncements have become increasingly unintelligible to the practitioners. But as managers need help, and as this help is not forthcoming from the theorists, it has fallen on management consultants to come up with practical propositions, in the form of recipes derived from intuitive and 'reasonable' concepts, drawn from experience and case studies, but alas based on limited hard evidence. This has given rise to many fashions in management, and like other fashions they come and go, generally leaving behind only an ephemeral impact on management practice. Their main benefit is that they encourage managers to question current organizational structures and procedures, to consider how they can be changed, and to fight against apathy and complacency. The danger of fashionable doctrines is that they become akin to faith-healing and the administered potions can lead to the adoption of what may be regarded as management mispractices, namely practices that are based on questionable beliefs and premises.

How is the gulf between theory and practice to be bridged and how can we ensure that future managers will be able to cope with the ever-growing dynamics and complexity of the industrial scene? It is generally accepted that this challenge lies with the business schools, though doubts have been expressed in recent years about their ability to fulfil this role. Some aspects of this important debate are covered in the last three chapters. They pose important challenges to designers of business school curricula, which aim at producing the needed trained managers of the future, but they also raise fundamental questions regarding the ethos of such schools and the kind of research and forward thinking that they should be engaged in.

This book is aimed at managers, management consultants and students of management. The topics and problems discussed here are meant to provoke the reader and make him (or her) think about the many issues involved and to question established doctrines and beliefs. If the book encourages some readers to adopt an iconoclastic attitude towards what they find in the literature and towards the premisses on which many management theories and practices are founded, then it will have achieved its purpose.

Samuel Eilon
1991

Acknowledgements

This book is a sequel to three earlier volumes (published by Pergamon Press), *Management Control* (1979), *Aspects of Management* (1979) and *Management Assertions and Aversions* (1985), though all three are self-contained and familiarity with the earlier volumes is not necessary before reading this one. Much of the material assembled here has appeared in a shortened form in editorials published in *Omega, the International Journal of Management Science*, and I am grateful to Pergamon Press for permission to use that material here.

I am grateful to many friends in the business and academic worlds who have stimulated my interest in the topics discussed in this volume. Above all, I am grateful to my wife Hannah, who has patiently read several re-drafts and – as always – made many valuable suggestions. I should stress, however, that any deficiencies in content and style are entirely my own.

CHAPTER 1

Structuring the unstructured

Order out of chaos

The managerial scene is epitomized by chaos. Managers are concerned with steering and controlling industrial and business systems in order to achieve certain ends, usually defined in terms of characteristic behaviour or a series of performance criteria. The behaviour and performance of the systems, whether their purpose is the production of physical goods or the provision of services, depend on numerous variables.

Many of these variables are completely outside the control of managers but are determined by external factors, such as competition, the general economic and political environment, legislation, or even the behaviour of other industrial and business systems. Within the vast array of variables that impinge on the behaviour of business systems, only a subset is amenable to change by managerial manipulation, which manifests itself in the form of specific actions: determining the appropriate mix and acquisition of resource inputs, planning the mix of outputs, allocating resources to those responsible for producing the outputs, and scheduling and coordinating activities with the available resources over a given time horizon.

Three factors further compound the complexity of the problems encountered by managers. First, freedom of managerial action is subject to many constraints, some of which are self-imposed: by higher managerial echelons on lower echelons (vertical constraints) in line with overall corporate policy, or by the fact that actions taken by some parts of the organization automatically diminish the freedom of manoeuvre of others (horizontal constraints). Other constraints are imposed by external agencies (such as legal requirements, health and safety standards, agreed terms of trade, market prices of input factors, and so on (Eilon 1979).

Secondly, many of the variables that affect the behaviour of business systems are interconnected, so that a change in one can trigger a chain reaction that affects many others. Consequently, it is often very difficult to ascertain clear cause-and-effect relationships; in many circumstances it is not even clear which is the cause and which is the effect. This difficulty is further exacerbated by the third factor, which is to do with the random nature of many variables and the functional relationships between them.

The result is a highly volatile mass of system attributes with various behavioural characteristics that often appear to be obscure and unpredictable. The task of management is to make sense of this chaos, and proceed to create order out of disorder. Most of the problems encountered by managers are unstructured, or at least this is how they are first perceived. It is by seeking to structure unstructured problems that managers can hope to develop consistent and reliable methods for tackling them. This quest for order is greatly assisted by modelling, the purpose of which is to enable managers to understand the behaviour and performance of the system under their responsibility and take action to control it.

The focus on decision making

Against this background, it is understandable that a vast literature has mushroomed during the last thirty years on the art and science of decision making, a subject that today remains as topical as ever. It was in 1960 that Herbert Simon wrote a slim volume entitled *The New Science of Management Decisions* (1960), in which he explored the decision-making process as an exercise in problem solving.

The crux of the manager's function, it is argued, is to make choices, and Simon happily uses the term 'decision making' as though it were synonymous with 'managing', so that when we come to study decisions, we should not focus on the moment when a final choice from several alternatives is made, but rather consider 'the whole lengthy and complex process of alerting, exploring and analysing that precede that final moment' (1960: 1). As he puts it,

Executives spend a large fraction of their time surveying the economic, technical, political, and social environment to identify new conditions that call for new actions. They probably spend an even larger fraction of their time, individually or with associates, seeking to invent, design and develop possible courses of action for handling situations where a decision is needed. They spend a small fraction of their time in choosing among alternative actions already developed to meet an identified problem and already analysed for their consequences.

These stages are highlighted by Simon as *intelligence* (in the military sense, namely information gathering), *design* and *choice*.

The decision-making process

A more detailed description of this process is shown in Figure 1.1, where the design stage is spelt out in some detail (Eilon 1979). The essence of this decision-making model is that it addresses itself to the following questions:

- Where are we now? *(information)*
- What is the cause for the current position? *(analysis)*
- Where do we want to get to? *(objectives)*
- How would we know whether we got there? *(measurement)*
- What alternative routes are open to us? *(modelling)*
- What are the costs, benefits and other consequences of each alternative? *(performance criteria and prediction of outcomes)*
- How do we choose? *(choice criteria)*

The answers to these questions need not be pursued and finalized in any particular sequence, so that the process may well become iterative, with feedback loops between the various boxes in the figure 1.1. As the process continues, the decision maker eventually becomes satisfied that information gathering and analysis have gone on for long enough for the viable alternative courses of action to be mapped out, or that time and cost constraints require the process to be curtailed, so that a final resolution (i.e. a choice between alternatives) must be made.

3

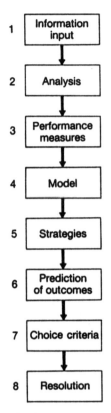

Figure 1.1 The decision process (Eilon 1979)

The manner in which this selection is carried out raises many issues, such as the criteria of choice, the degree to which choice may be said to be rational, and the question of what is meant by the decision maker being 'free to choose' under these circumstances. All these issues have been the subject of numerous discussions in the literature (see, for example, Ofstad 1961; Eilon 1979) and need not concern us here.

Instead, let us turn our attention to the decision process that precedes the final choice, though it should be recognized that in reality the process of management does not terminate as abruptly as Figure 1.1 may suggest, and many managers spend most of their time in implementation and execution, as well as in monitoring and evaluation, the outcome of which often demands adjustments to plans and even changes in direction in the light of changing circumstances. Simon is obviously aware of the need to take account of the task of carrying out decisions, but believes that execution is itself a decision-making activity (1960: 3–4), so that changing conditions generate fresh activities in Simon's stages of intelligence gathering and design; in other words, the process depicted in the figure 1.1 is not a 'one-off' exercise, but permeates throughout the managerial activity, both at the planning phase and during implementation and execution.

Routine and non-routine decisions

How well equipped are managers to make decisions? Leaving aside such issues as personality, experience and attitude to risk (all of which have a significant bearing on the style and tempo of the managerial process), we need to consider the types of problems that the decision maker is required to solve. Simon proposes two main types of decisions:

- *Programmed decisions* – these are characterized as repetitive and routine, so that well-defined procedures have been (or can be) developed to handle the problems as they occur.
- *Non-programmed decisions* – these are novel and unstructured, so that there are no prescribed procedures or sets of rules that the decision maker can readily resort to.

Simon's reason for distinguishing between programmed and non-programmed decisions is his belief that different techniques are used to handle the two types: programmed decisions operate on the basis of standard operating procedures, or based on OR (Operational Research) and computer models, whereas non-programmed decisions cater for 'one-shot, ill-structured novel policy' problems and traditionally rely on judgement and intuition or heuristic methods, and that approach is characterized by 'general problem-solving processes'. Although Simon accepts that the distinction between the two types is a matter of convenience ('hoping that the reader will remind himself from time to time that the world is mostly gray with only a few spots of pure black or white'), he is at pains to emphasize the fundamental difference (as he sees it) between the two types of decisions, and consequently between the executives assigned to handle them (1960: 5).

> There is no reason to expect that a man who has acquired a fairly high level of personal skill in decision-making activity will have a correspondingly high skill in designing efficient decision-making systems. To imagine that there is such a connection is like supposing that a man who is a good weight lifter can therefore design cranes. The skill of designing and maintaining the modern decision-making systems we call organizations are less intuitive skills. Hence they are even more susceptible to training than the skills of personal decision making.

Now, whether the analogy of the weight lifter and crane designer is at all appropriate is open to some doubt, but the main message of Simon's discussion, that managers need different attributes when dealing with different types of problems, is well taken.

However, rather than consider programmed v. non-programmed decisions, it may be preferable to categorize more extensively the types of problems that managers encounter. In order to gain a better understanding of what 'routine' means, reference needs to be made to the attributes of *frequency* and *replication*.

> The frequency with which a given decision has to be made within a given space of time is a measure of the repetitiveness of the task of the decision maker. Replication is to do with the uniformity in the definition of the problems ... the greater the variations in these problems the lower the level of replication. Thus, decisions with high replication and high frequency are *routine decisions*, while those with low replication and low frequency may be called *ad hoc* at the other end of the 'routine scale'
>
> (Eilon 1979: 33)

The simple matrix in Table 1.1 shows the two ends of the scale represented by cells 1 and 4 respectively, and while the designation as to what is meant by 'high' and 'low' is somewhat arbitrary, the matrix suggests the degree to which a trend towards programmable decisions may be expected. It is clear that the more routine the

Table 1.1   Types of problems

		Frequency	
		High	Low
Replication	High	1	2
	Low	3	4

problem, the more amenable it is to be handled by standard procedures, to be delegated to lower echelons in the managerial hierarchy, even to clerks who merely have to follow a rule book, and ultimately to computers programmed to identify the relevant case in a decision table and implement the corresponding pre-scribed course of action. At the other end of the scale, in the case of the *ad hoc* novel problems, such delegation is less feasible, because problem-solving procedures have not been developed for the purpose.

Mechanizing the decision process

Thus, the matrix in Table 1.1 provides a useful guide in facing the question of how far to proceed with automatic computer proces-sing as an aid or substitute to conventional decision making: problems in cell 1 are the first candidates for such treatment. Their high degree of replication suggests a stable and recognizable structure, so that they become amenable to systematic definition and standard presentation.

These qualities, coupled with a clear determination of the solution domain and predetermined criteria for ordering possible solutions, imply that a mechanistic solution procedure can be devised for a prescribed sequence of actions and responses, and this procedure can then be automatically followed whenever a problem in this class is encountered. The high frequency of problems in cell 1 suggests that the benefits afforded by a programmed and automated decision procedure (speed of response, accuracy, consistency, reliability, low cost of processing) would be frequently enjoyed, and thus become a convincing economic argument for developing and implementing the appropriate procedure.

In cell 2 the position is less clear-cut. The high level of replication still underlines the technical case for programmed decisions, but the low frequency with which these problems occur suggests that the economic justification for developing programmed decisions depends on the envisaged cost saving and on other benefits in operational terms.

Problems in cell 4 appear to be least amenable for programming (but more about this issue later), both from a technical and an economic viewpoint, but it is cell 3 that presents the most intriguing challenge to management. The low level of replication of problems in this cell suggests that they are ill structured, perhaps with many unpredictable and poorly defined characteristics, that even their objectives and performance measures are not clear, so that the solution domain needs to be ascertained afresh every time a problem in this category presents itself. This is the area that, on the face of it, seems destined to remain the province of intuitive decision making, relying largely on the experience and flair of individual decision makers.

And yet, the high frequency of problems in cell 3 points to the potential significant economic and other benefits that might accrue from developing methods that encapsulate human experience and intuition, thereby highlighting the rationale for current work in the field of expert systems coupled with so-called artificial intelligence. This is also where the main promise of DSS (Decision Support Systems) lies and where a concerted research effort is currently being invested, the prevailing premiss being that even if the decision process cannot be programmed in its entirety on a computer, a man–machine system can be developed to take advantage of both partners, the experience and (so far) certain undefined problem-solving skills of man, coupled with the reliability, speed and dogged consistency of the machine. Already thirty years ago Simon hinted at the development of DSS by advocating what he called 'heuristic problem solving techniques applied to: (a) training human decision makers, (b) constructing heuristic computer programs' (1960: 8).

The matrix in Table 1.1 categorizes problems in four discrete cells but (as hinted earlier) this presentation is merely a matter of convenience; in practice, strict lines of demarcation between the categories would be difficult to draw. It is this feature that renders the commonly accepted distinction between structured and un-structured decisions less clear-cut than is generally assumed. It conjures up the notion that the very approach to problem solving is fundamentally different for non-programmed decisions compared with programmed decisions. But in practice it appears that, when faced with a new situation, which he (she) has not encountered previously, the manager tries to draw on his (her) experience with other situations, to rely on analogies and inferences, and generally search for familiar signposts as he gropes his way along an un-familiar route.

In short, when faced with an unstructured problem, the decision maker's natural reaction is to treat it as if it were structured and to adopt whatever systematic analytical tools are to hand to design a methodology for handling the situation. As Simon put it:

> One thing we have known about nonprogrammed decision making is that it can be improved somewhat by training in orderly thinking. In addition to the very specific habits one can acquire for doing very specific things, one can acquire the habit – when confronted with a vague and difficult situation – of asking 'what is the problem?' We can even construct rather generalized operating procedures for decision making, [for example the use of] a check-list of things to consider in analysing a problem (1960: 11).

This tendency is confirmed by empirical observations, such as in a study by Mintzberg *et al.* (1976: 247) who say: 'Thus, we conclude from the studies of individual decision making that decision pro-cesses are programmable even if they are not in fact programmed.' These observations lead Mintzberg to suggest that managers develop and follow a *decision recognition routine*, to assimilate information relating to situations that involve opportunities or crises, and a *diagnosis routine*, to evaluate this information prior to considera-tion of possible solutions. The detailed stages of this decision process are discussed at some length by Mintzberg *et al.* and they are reminiscent of the sequential approach advocated in OR text-books, even though that approach is intended for structured prob-lems that ostensibly belong to cell 1.

Categories of decisions

All this suggests that the prime difference between structured and unstructured decisions lies in the degree of clarity with which the decision maker perceives his (her) task: clarity as to what a particular problem is all about, the environment in which it is set, and the objective that he is supposed to pursue. These issues are obviously affected by the frequency with which problems arise and by their degree of replication, as suggested in Table 1.1. The main categories of decision-making situations are proposed in Table 1.2 with special reference to the definition of goals and to the availability and type of information provided.

The first three categories in Table 1.2 are well covered in the literature and concern *decision making under deterministic conditions, under risk and under uncertainty, respectively.* The first relates to the case where the objective is well defined and where all the information that the decision maker needs is fully available, whether it is in relation to operating conditions, resources costs or constraints, as well as information on all the possible courses of

Table 1.2 Four categories of decisions

		Goals	Information	Examples
A	Decision making under deterministic conditions	Well defined	Fully available, deterministic variables and outcomes	LP models, TSP, layout and scheduling problems, theory of games models
B	Decision making under risk	Well defined	Fully available, stochastic variables and outcomes	Inventory problems queuing models
C	Decision making under uncertainty	Well defined	Incomplete	Capital investmental appraisal
D	Decision making under ambiguity	Unclear	Incomplete	Diversification, new products, organizational design

actions and their respective pay-offs (or, at least, the means by which these pay-offs can be ascertained). Furthermore, all the data for problems in the first category are deterministic.

These conditions do not necessarily render problems in this category simplistic or trivial. For example, the travelling salesman problem (TSP for short), where the objective is to minimize the total distance travelled in visiting a given array of locations, is highly structured and deterministic, yet mathematically it is a complex combinatorial problem and the optimal solution, even for a problem of moderate size, is difficult to find.

The same is true of layout problems, which aim to locate facilities in a production centre with the objective of minimizing handling costs, and of production scheduling problems, which require a scheduler to determine sequences of operations subject to complex constraints on timing and availability of resources. Chess and most models found in textbooks on the theory of games are further examples of problems belonging to this category. Even linear programming models, which are typical of highly structured deterministic problems and for which computer packages are widely available, can become mathematically intricate when non-linear relationships and/or integer variables are introduced. It is not surprising, therefore, that much of the effort in developing programmed decision methods in recent years has been directed to problems in this category.

The second category in Table 1.2, category B, again involves problems with clear objectives and complete information. The only difference between these problems and those in the previous category is that here future events are subject to chance. The assumption, though, is that this chance can be quantified in probabilistic terms, so that every possible event or outcome has a probability value attached to it, and that this information is known to the decision maker. He does appreciate, therefore, that any decision involves a risk and that the consequences of bad luck may at times be catastrophic. In making a decision he must weigh these risks against the attraction of a possible high pay-off (which is usually associated with a relatively low probability), and this consideration leads to attitudes of risk aversion v. risk taking. The performance measures adopted in these circumstances involve expected values, range of probable outcomes, probability of loss or breakdown, probability of achieving a minimum pre-specified level of performance, and so on. Although the final choice between several courses of action may not be as clear-cut as for problems in category A, here too there is a wide scope for programmed decision making, at least up to the point when the final choice is made.

The next category in Table 1.2, category C, concerns decision making under uncertainty, where information about future events is incomplete. A good example is that of capital investment appraisal, where many variables which may affect the profitability of a project are difficult to predict, such as price, production costs, volume, interest rates, the resale value of the plant at some future date, and so on. Although many factors relating to the future may be imponderable, the methodology for analysing a capital investment proposal can (at least, in principle) be programmed, so that for a *given set of assumptions and performance criteria*, a range of possible outcomes can be computed (such as the distribution of net present value, or internal rate of return). The computational approaches may either rely on techniques employed for decision making under risk (in other words, uncertainty is formulated as a set of possible scenarios, or as a set of probability values for alternative outcomes) or by risk simulation (where many scenarios are generated by sampling from hypothetical distributions of variables). The computational results, coupled with appropriate sensitivity analyses, then provide the manager with a basis for making his decision.

The fourth category in Table 1.2 again involves incomplete information about the environment and future possible outcomes, but here the objectives of the decision process are not entirely clear. This class of problems calls for *decision making under ambiguity* (a term suggested by Mintzberg *et al.* for situations where 'almost nothing is given or easily determined', to be distinguished from *decision making under uncertainty*, 'where alternatives are given even if their consequences are not' (1976: 251)). Category D in Table 1.2 represents the most unstructured of the problems discussed so far. As intimated above, the natural tendency of a decision maker faced with such problems is to find some reference point in his past experience, on which to build an approach to design and scan alternative choices. In the absence of clear-cut objectives, he develops his own, explicitly or implicitly; in the absence of information, he conjures up 'reasonable' scenarios. Whether he systematically explores a decision tree or whether his reactions are spontaneous and intuitive depends not only on his personality and aptitude, but on the time available for the decision to be made.

The categorization of problems and decisions in Tables 1.1 and 1.2 is obviously incomplete. It tells us nothing about the way problems emerge, or whether they require a one-off verdict ('buy X', 'accept offer Y', 'set production at rate Z for the next month'), as opposed to a continuous decision process involving a sequence of many interacting decisions (for example, in building a plant, where there are recurring opportunities to rectify past errors or to adapt plans in the light of new information). Nor does the categorization in the two tables concern itself with the time scale of required responses, or indeed even with the relative importance of the problems that the decision maker has to tackle. All these issues obviously have a bearing on assigning priorities to problems, on the amount of time that can be devoted to them, on the degree of delegation that may be contemplated, and on developing procedures that are thought to be appropriate for monitoring, evaluation and control (before, during and after decisions are made).

The challenge of strategic decisions

The foregoing discussion explains why management theorists and management consultants argue that further research needs to be done to refine and elaborate the proposed classification of decision-making processes. What does emerge from Tables 1.1 and 1.2 is that a simple distinction between structured and unstructured problems or between programmed and non-programmed decisions is too crude for a proper understanding of the issues involved.

There are, admittedly, at one end of the scale highly structured, well-defined, routine problems, and at the other end completely unstructured problems. But by examining the categories in-between, and by observing the manner in which they are handled in practice, we conclude that the methodology of decision makers is to structure the unstructured, namely to construct problem-solving procedures that rely heavily on experience with more structured

13

situations. This, after all, is the essence of all learning processes, where knowledge of the known equips us to face the unknown. In this context, therefore, non-programmed decisions today may well become programmed tomorrow, as evidenced by the growing impact of DSS.

In this chapter we highlighted the search for structuring the decision-making process by delineating common features between problems encountered in business, so that a common array of models and common methods for solving them can be outlined. This search for structure is not confined to the later stages of the decision-making process in Figure 1.1 or to problems in the early categories in Table 1.2.

As suggested earlier, routine and highly structured problems can be programmed and delegated to the lower echelons in the managerial hierarchy. By contrast, strategic problems tend to belong to category D in Table 1.2, where executives and analysts ask themselves questions about corporate objectives, performance criteria and determinants of corporate success or failure. It is understandable that in their desire to offer advice and guidance, academics and management consultants keep searching for ways in which to structure and model ill-defined situations. As we shall see in the following chapters, this quest raises many conceptual problems which have important practical ramifications, and some of the methods that have been applied in the business world raise serious questions of relevance and validity.

References

Eilon, S. 1979. *Management Control.* Oxford: Pergamon Press.
Mintzberg, H., Raisinghani, D. and Theoret, A. 1976. The structure of 'unstructured' decision processes. *Administrative Science Quarterly* 21: 246–75.
Ofstad, H. 1961. *An Inquiry into the Freedom of Decisions.* London: Allen & Unwin.
Simon, H. A. 1960. *The New Science of Management Decision.* New York: Harper & Row.

CHAPTER 2

Mission incomplete

The mission statement

The higher you go in the organization hierarchy the greater is the need to engage in what were described in the last chapter as unstructured decisions. In contrast to experience at the lower managerial echelons, problems encountered by senior managers are less likely to replicate the past, they are often ill-defined, they are associated with ambiguous objectives and involve a high level of uncertainty. It is not surprising that a great deal of effort is invested in trying to delineate a coherent framework within which executives can methodically analyse these problems as part of their task to manage and control the complex systems for which they are responsible. One such area, for which a methodological framework has been advocated, concerns the very top echelon of the organization. In this chapter we examine its rationale and indicate some of its shortcomings.

Textbooks on business policy, strongly reinforced by consultants on corporate strategy, keep hammering home the message that the Chairman/CEO (Chief Executive Officer) of an enterprise and his fellow directors must have a clear vision of specific ultimate corporate goals as an expression of their ambition for consummate achievements. If you don't have an ultimate goal, so the argument goes, you don't know where you are going; and if you don't know where you are going, you cannot have a structured performance evaluation, you cannot plan the utilization of your financial resources effectively, you become easily side-tracked by short-term considerations, and – last but not least – you cannot provide a sense of direction and challenge to your managers and to the workforce. People strive for achievement when they have a clear goal, and they derive satisfaction from being able to make progress towards it.

This is why the CEO must have a vision, which he (or she) must share with other members of the top hierarchy in the organization. The vision is created as part of a strategy analysis process, as described briefly in Figure 2.1, which aims at having a full understanding of the strengths and weaknesses of the enterprise in relation to the market and to the main competitors. The process is an iterative one, as suggested by the feedback arrows in the diagram, so that every step benefits from knowledge gained both in previous and subsequent steps.

Once the vision of the CEO and the board is created, it needs to cascade down to the lower echelons through the declaration of a

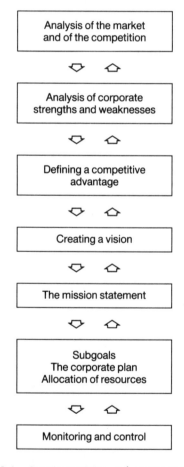

Figure 2.1   Creating a vision and a mission statement

'*mission statement*'. This is then followed by the formulation of a corporate strategy, which maps out the actions and the resources needed to convert aspirations into reality, and the overall corporate plan is thus cast against a time scale with bench-marks for monitoring and review (for a further discussion of the managerial control process see Eilon (1979); we return to this subject in subsequent chapters of this book).

A well-developed corporate plan generates a set of specific targets for each part of the organization, so that every division, every department, every section, and indeed every individual, knows exactly what tasks and performance are expected at specified time periods. Furthermore, all the subgoals within the organization need to be compatible with, and form integral parts of, the overall corporate goal.

The mission statement has a dual function. First, it is a visionary declaration of intent, designed to lift the spirit of the managerial hierarchy and to set a challenge for the enterprise as a whole; secondly, it provides a framework within which current and future activities can be planned and executed. In short, it is a super corporate blueprint. Once the mission statement is ratified by the board, the detailed exercise of allocating responsibilities and resources can proceed in a systematic fashion (this issue is discussed further in Chapter 13).

So far so good. The mission statement is the first visible step in the development of a rational management-control process, starting at the strategic level before tactical planning and execution can be embarked upon. It all sounds so obvious, and so simple. Senior managers arc easily persuaded that this recipe is bound to ensure clarity of purpose and foster a spirit of teamwork among all their managers. Consequently, many CEOs embark on this road enthusiastically, only to be disappointed by the outcome, which somehow does not measure up to the initial expectations. The reason for this shortfall is that composing a mission statement is neither obvious nor simple, as the following real example will illustrate.

An example

The example is taken from a well-known company in the engineering industry. In order to ensure that a consistent message is transmitted to the employees, the shareholders, the customers, the suppliers, the banks and financial analysts, in short to all those who have any interest in the company, the CEO agonized for a long while before producing a mission statement that was circulated to all the employees and was also included in the company's annual report. The statement (which is reproduced here almost intact) consists of six aims, and these are listed in Table 2.1.

Table 2.1 An example of a mission statement

1 The primary aims of our Group are to provide a sound investment for our shareholders and also worthwhile job prospects for our employees.
2 Our objectives are customer satisfaction, real growth in earnings per share, and a competitive return on capital employed.
3 The business policy of the Group is to provide good quality and high added-value products for markets throughout the world.
4 Management of business operations is decentralized into Divisions, each responsible to the Board for growth, financial performance, asset management and employment practices.
5 We aim to have a highly skilled, well informed and competitively compensated workforce, who are encouraged to seek investment and career progression within the Group.
6 Our task is to establish the Group as a market-driven, cost-efficient, achievement-orientated company.

Bearing in mind that this was the first time in the history of the company that such a declaration of intent had ever been explicitly and publicly stated, it was widely acclaimed, and its initial impact on the managerial structure was remarkable. The declaration was regarded as an inspiring and challenging message, and the first reaction of managers on reading it was decidedly positive. Notice that the declaration is not merely an expression of a general aspiration 'to be successful', but that it incorporates several specific goals. Leaving aside the question of whether they are all equally important, or whether they are listed in the right order, the declaration makes an attempt to delineate clearly the major desirable operational and performance criteria, which the CEO and his fellow directors have identified as important, and thereby it sets the scene for the various parts of the enterprise to plan their activities accordingly.

The scrutiny

After a short while, individual managers began to scrutinize the mission statement more closely and each began to ask himself the inevitable questions. How do I fit in the overall grand design? What does the corporate mission precisely mean with respect to my own job and for those reporting to me? What exactly are we supposed to achieve, and when? And how would we know whether we have achieved what is expected of us or not?

In order to have a better appreciation of these questions, let us examine the stated mission in greater detail. To begin with, we note that the declaration of intent is not expressed as a single goal, but consists of six statements involving several goals. The first statement attempts to placate two interested parties, namely the shareholders (who look for an adequate return on their investment) and the employees (who wish to have rewarding jobs and good career prospects). The second also covers a mixture of things, in that it deals with yet another interested party, the customer, as well as specifying two corporate financial criteria (those highlighted are earnings per share and return on capital) that are very likely to exercise the minds of shareholders and financial analysts. The third statement deals with product quality (showing again a concern for the customer) and puts emphasis on high added-value activities. The fourth indicates a degree of decentralization and demands accountability to the board for all managerial activities. The fifth returns to the employees and emphasizes skill, knowledge, remuneration and commitment. Finally, the declaration concludes with the need to satisfy the market, to be efficient (in cost terms) and to meet targets.

This chopping and changing of the orientation in the mission statement (which is fairly typical of similar declarations encountered in many enterprises) is somewhat disconcerting. It stems from the fact that, as indicated above, there are many parties with vested interests in the wellbeing and performance of the enterprise. For the sake of clarity, it might have been better to delineate these parties and deal with them one by one in the mission statement in a systematic fashion. Alternatively, the statement could have concentrated on the functions within the organization (finance, product policy, marketing and distribution, manufacturing, etc), and proceeded to designate performance goals to each function.

When questioned on this point, the CEO (who was the main author of the mission statement) argued that this is merely a matter of style and presentation, though to an outside observer the formulation of the aims and their sequence gives a clue about the main concerns and anxieties of the CEO and his colleagues.

The mixture of external and internal audiences, for whom the statement is promulgated, is not only intended to satisfy the needs and perceptions of its diverse readers, but to highlight the fact that this multitude of interests inevitably generates different expectations and different perceptions of priorities, and thereby highlights the need for many performance criteria. As a result, the statement cannot have a single sharp focus and it is not surprising, therefore, that coherence and consistency have to suffer.

What do the goals mean?

Leaving aside the format, the wording and the style of this mission statement, important though they may well be, it is interesting to note that, in common with many other mission statements designed to cater for a wide audience, they have to rely on generalities. Every single goal and aspiration mentioned in this statement is vague. There is no indication of what level of achievement should be aimed at, or what would be regarded as satisfactory. Consider, for example, the following questions:

On financial objectives:

- What is a 'sound investment' for shareholders?
- What is a 'competitive return on capital employed?'
- What e.p.s. (earnings per share) should the company aim for?
- What growth rate in e.p.s. would be acceptable?

On the customers:

- What is the meaning of 'customer satisfaction'?
- How is the customer service to be defined and measured?

On the quality of the product:

- How should quality be measured?

- What level should be aimed at?
- Should high quality be produced at any price?

On the employees:

- What level of remuneration would be regarded as 'competitive'?
- What are 'worthwhile job prospects'?
- What is meant by 'highly skilled, well-informed workforce'?

And so on. The mission statement does not provide any answers to these questions, nor should you expect it to. Its purpose is merely to outline broad guidance, to give notice to all concerned that the CEO and the board mean business, that they are intent on moving forward to improve corporate performance, and thereby to provide an overall challenge to the organization and inspire its employees. It is precisely because the statement has a wide audience that it tends to avoid any mention of quantitative measures or become too specific in defining goals (indeed, definitions are usually bypassed), let alone give an indication of how the goals should be linked or reconciled, and how they should be pursued in practice.

The universal mission statement

And this is why, once a mission statement has been promulgated, it is very difficult to 'update' it, since the main sentiments expressed in the statement remain valid year after year. Admittedly, if an organization undergoes drastic changes in structure and managerial style following a change in the top leadership, then attempts to revise or rewrite the mission statement would aim to reflect these changes and perhaps put stress on a new set of priorities.

More often than not, however, the general nature of the statement makes it almost immutable and widely acceptable. Indeed, it is interesting to note that in the above example, the industrial sector to which the company belongs is not even mentioned, nor is the size of the company or the range of products produced. There is no indication of its geographical location or whether its business is centred on a national market or is international, whether the operations are labour-intensive or rely on heavy capital expenditure, whether the product involves conventional technology or is dependent on active R&D (research and development) and innovation. In fact, the mission statement in the example in Table 2.1 could apply to any enterprise, whether it is engaged in manufacturing or providing a service. It is a general framework within which any decent and responsible management would wish to operate.

At the risk of depriving strategy consultants of their livelihood, one might even be tempted to say that it should be possible to find a form of words that would be universally applicable and to which only one or two phrases would have to be added to 'customize' it, in order to reflect the priorities, the special characteristics or the needs of a particular organization. For example, a CEO may wish it to be generally known that he aims for his company to become No. 1 in its industrial sector in terms of sales volume or profitability, or that he intends to excel in the design and manufacture of a particular product range, or to achieve a minimum annual sales of x billion before the end of the decade. But all these additions are just frills to elaborate on what is essentially a common aspiration denominator.

In the main, a mission statement recognizes the truism that an enterprise has to satisfy the needs and expectations of three parties in order to become (or remain) successful, namely:

- the shareholders and providers of capital,
- the customers, and
- the employees.

Except for circumstances where some of these parties are irrelevant (for example, when the enterprise is not a publicly quoted company and has plenty of cash, or when market demand greatly exceeds supply to the extent that the wishes of the customer may be ignored), all three parties need to be 'kept happy', and this is the general message that the mission statement attempts to convey. In this respect, therefore, there is little to differentiate one mission statement from another. They are all, so to speak, in favour of motherhood, compassion and exemplary behaviour.

And this is the reason why the mission statement is generally received with approbation, even enthusiasm, when it is first released. To avoid the sense of disappointment that may subsequently develop, it is essential for the CEO to appreciate that the mission statement is not an end in itself, but merely an expression of an overall vision.

Having announced his destination, the CEO then needs to consider how to deploy his resources in order to get there. In order to achieve a financial performance that would satisfy investors and financial analysts, it is necessary to set out the specific criteria that have to be met and then proceed with a plan of action, showing how aspirations can be converted into reality. In order to satisfy the customers, it is necessary to fully understand what they need, how these needs can be met, what the competitors are up to, and what it would take to win customers away from them. In order to satisfy the employees, it is necessary to institute reward systems that compare well with competing employers in the labour market, to provide training and career development, and above all to implement programmes that would encourage employees to behave like owners, in terms of their involvement and commitment (this theme is further developed in Chapters 13 and 14).

Conclusion

Many enterprises have been in business for so long that their senior executives take their comfortable existence for granted. And then changes in the economic and political climate take place that upset the status quo and threaten the market equilibrium. Analysis of corporate strategy has become one of the fastest growing activities of management consultants in recent years and it is common practice for CEOs and their senior executives to seek counsel in these turbulent times.

For some reason, it comes as a great revelation to many of them when they are confronted by some fundamental questions:

- What business are you in?
- What are you trying to achieve?
- What vision do you have about the future of your enterprise?
- Where would you like the organization to be in five years' time?
- Do your colleagues and subordinates understand and share this vision?

- How effective are you in communicating your aspirations to the managerial echelons and the rest of the workforce?
- What mechanisms have been instituted to define and promulgate these aspirations to others?

These senior executives have been immersed in the day-to-day demands of their jobs for so long that they have not given much thought to these fundamental questions. Some may not even appreciate their importance. Being able to detach themselves from their daily chores and spend time with the consultants on these issues is seen as a welcome opportunity to stimulate the managerial hierachy and revitalize the organization. In the light of mounting external pressures, this is seen by many as an opportunity that should not be missed.

And the first thing that the strategy consultants urge them to do is to create a corporate vision and formulate a mission statement. Where many CEOs fail is in thinking that the mission statement is an end in itself, that it is a panacea that would solve all their problems, instead of realizing that it is, in fact, only the beginning of a long and hard grind.

The intriguing question that they ought to ask themselves is: If the process of searching for a vision culminates in a mission statement which is essentially the same for a very large number of enterprises, what is it that makes some more successful than others? This is a question that we shall turn to in the next chapter.

Reference

Eilon, S. 1979. *Management Control.* Oxford: Pergamon Press.

CHAPTER 3

Determinants of corporate performance

What makes a company successful?

As suggested in the last chapter, the mission statement serves as a stimulant for many questions that need to be asked about the way in which an enterprise should be managed in order to achieve success. A key function in the management control process is monitoring the operations performed by various parts of the organization, coupled with analysis of performance at the corporate level. The purpose of this control process is twofold: first, the senior executives need to understand why the company has performed in the way that it has, and secondly, they constantly wish to explore alternative courses of action that would improve the performance.

Associated with the design of suitable monitoring and control processes are other key issues that affect corporate performance, such as management style and philosophy, corporate aspirations and priorities, not to mention organizational structure. Each of these factors is likely to have a significant impact on operations and on performance, and it is natural for managers and analysts to seek to understand the nature of these influences.

Consider the following question: given two companies belonging to the same industrial sector and operating in the same environment, what makes one more successful than the other? To put it differently, can the less successful company emulate the philosophy and practices of its successful rival and thereby achieve the same level of results? Can one learn from the experience of others and deduce causal relationships that determine corporate performance?

Before we proceed, we need to clarify briefly what is meant by 'success', and from whose point of view. Employees will naturally measure success by the level of their remuneration, conditions of work, and security of employment. Managers will judge success by comparing the actual performance of their departments with the levels of performance expected of them. Customers, suppliers, investors and creditors, all have their own interests and hence their own criteria. It therefore follows that what may be seen as successful by some may well be regarded in a different light by others. For the purpose of our discussion here we shall confine the term 'success' to refer to corporate performance as viewed by financial analysts and commentators, namely performance which is indicated by conventional financial criteria (such as sales revenue, profit, return on investment, relative share price, etc.), without highlighting any single one in particular (we shall return to the question of the relevance of these criteria and their compatibility with each other in later chapters).

Clearly, the intriguing question of which are the major determinants of corporate performance is of great interest to managers and industrial commentators. If such determinants could be identified, they would serve two purposes. First, they would offer a diagnostic framework to explain historical corporate performance and suggest reasons for companies progressing at different rates. Secondly, they would form the foundation for a normative model to guide future managerial action aiming at improving performance. These issues are, therefore, not merely the subject of academic curiosity, but have significant implications for daily practice.

Many thousands of people are constantly wrestling with these problems: students taking courses in business policy in business schools, research workers, financial analysts, business executives, and, not least, management consultants. Some have only a transitory interest in the subject, perhaps stimulated by a particular problem that demands attention, others have made it a lifetime occupation. How do they go about studying the many issues involved?

The use of case studies

Inevitably, they turn to case studies and resort to comparisons: If two companies differ only in one definable characteristic, all other things being equal, then it is tempting to assign the cause for different performance levels to that characteristic, and the credentials of such a hypothesis are naturally strengthened as more corroborative evidence is unravelled.

The problem, however, is that in reality all things are never equal. The economic and social environment, for one, is ever changing, so that comparing two companies (or a company with itself) at different time periods is always subject to the distinct possibility that changes in the environment have been the root cause of differences in the companies' fortunes: government economic policy, changes in demand, competition, interest and currency exchange rates, prices and input costs, variations in product specifications, as well as changes in operating procedures – they all raise doubts about the scope and validity of comparative case studies, and hence about the confidence with which a single variable can be delineated for the construction or testing of a hypothesis for our purposes. To eliminate these effects of time, case studies need to be confined to the same time period, but even then it is virtually impossible to identify companies which are identical in all respects but one, so as to permit the conclusion that the one difference in their make-up is the real and only cause of differences in their performance.

This weakness in the case-study methodology is well known and has always been of great concern to research workers and analysts, but in their defence it has been argued that there is no better way. A company is not a mechanical system that can be isolated in a laboratory and subjected to a systematic series of experiments in order to establish causal relationships. Experiments in the business world, where they are conducted, tend to be rather constrained in scope (for example, to production methods, marketing techniques, advertising and pricing campaigns), so that their results (however valuable for specific operational purposes) cannot aspire to provide a complete diagnosis or explanation even in particular instances, let alone form the basis for a generalized theory. Unlike many physical experiments in a laboratory, an argument about a hypothesis on business performance cannot be settled by a single 'crucial' test, and inevitably one needs to have a welter of case studies from which to extract evidence in defence of particular propositions.

As a result, an extensive case-study literature has grown in recent years, with variegated accounts of almost every conceivable complexion, some purely anecdotal with no pretensions of contributing to theory, others more structured in their data collection and analysis. Inevitably, many assertions and conclusions can be (and have been) put forward as to which is the most important and dominant factor that determines corporate performance, as the following examples illustrate.

1 The Great Man Theory

This theory postulates that the combination of qualities of drive and leadership of the man or woman at the top is what counts. He or she 'sets the tone' and dictates the managerial style throughout the organization, thereby affecting the commitment of all employees and the thrust with which they pursue the goals of the enterprise. The level of delegation, ability to respond to customer needs and changes in the market-place, internal communications, innovation and risk taking – all these are qualities that tend to be nurtured or suppressed by a strong personality at the helm, and it is not surprising, therefore, that business analysts often scrutinize the qualities of chief executives, trying to explain why companies in the same industrial sector exhibit different rates of change in their financial performance. The Great Man Theory has naturally led many research workers to write detailed biographies of leaders, including prominent captains of industry, and to embark on extensive studies of leadership qualities. In particular, there has been a lively debate on whether leaders are born or bred, since this is a central issue in the design and philosophy of business school programmes and has led to a profusion of leadership courses.

2 The Technology Dominance Theory

Adherents to the Technology Dominance Theory argue that corporate wellbeing is primarily affected by technology, which overshadows all other considerations. A company that adopts and exploits the most advanced technology in manufacturing plants, in control and in administration, is more likely to beat the competition on the efficiency and cost front, and thereby enhance the prospects for the company becoming more successful. This is why it is important to invest in R&D and to remain in the forefront of technology innovation and implementation.

3 The Product Dominance Theory

The proposition here is that the crucial factor for success is the product (or service), its novelty, its uniqueness in the market, its specifications, its quality, and the range of models (or variations) in which it is offered in order to provide customer choice. The corollary is that new demand for goods and services can be created by product innovation and design, and in this respect this proposition mirrors the normative conclusions of the Technology Dominance Theory, namely that the company needs to devote substantial resources to R&D and product design, and to be committed to launching new products and regularly upgrading existing ones

4 The Market Dominance Theory

If you start with the premiss that without customers the company has no basis for continued existence, then the essence of the Market Dominance Theory becomes self-evident: the company should be market-oriented, totally attuned to the customer's needs and fully aware of what the competition is up to. Thus, market research and market intelligence, aggressive promotion techniques, and attention to such matters as price, packaging, after-sales service, presentation and delivery dates naturally predominate management's thinking. Adherents to this philosophy are primarily concerned with sales volumes and market share. Consequently, they advocate that major resources be allocated to employing high-quality (and highly paid) staff in the marketing and sales function.

5 The Productivity Factor

To be competitive against products of similar design and quality, the company needs to attain low unit costs, which imply efficient use of resources and high productivity ratios (of output per unit of resource input). A company that manages to improve its productivity can afford to cut its selling prices, thus stimulate further demand for its products, increase sales revenue and achieve higher profit-

ability. The purposes of improved technology and greater productivity are the same, but the means of achieving this objective may
not be. The former sees increased productivity as the natural
outcome of technology, whereas the latter does not necessarily
ascribe higher productivity to the introduction of improved manufacturing hardware, but may wish to bring it about by the introduction of more efficient manufacturing methods, a new production
planning and control system, more effective training of employees,
new incentive schemes, and so on.

6 *The Economies of Scale Factor*

As new plant and machinery require increasing levels of capital
expenditure, higher production volumes are needed to absorb the
ensuing increase in depreciation and overhead costs. This trend is
particularly evident in industries that are dependent on capital-
intensive plants, where the introduction of new technology and the
high costs of new product innovation involve substantial financial
outlays. As a result, a large company engaged in large-volume
manufacture tends to enjoy a unit-cost advantage compared with a
smaller competitor, and in many industries economies of scale are
crucial for companies to remain in business. Although the larger
company may suffer from the risk of organizational atrophy (as a
result of growing bureaucracy, risk aversion, complacency, slow
exploitation of innovations, perceived loss of individual identity,
and general increase in inertia), it is argued that effective competition in world markets can only be realized once the company can
attain a minimum critical mass and benefit from the advantage of
economies of scale.

7 *The Organizational Structure Factor*

The adherents of the Organizational Structure School believe that
the all-important ingredient for a company to be successful is the
way it is organized to meet its missions, to ensure that its
constituent parts all pull in the same direction, and that demarcation of functions and responsibilities avoids gaps and unnecessary
overlaps. The organization structure needs, of course, to take
account of technology, company size, market conditions, and

geographical dispersion of facilities and product destination, as well as aspirations for growth and future developments. However, a structure that serves well one set of circumstances may be less appropriate in others and may be less conducive to achieving corporate success.

Dominant factors and interactions

This sample of postulates (there are many others) is typical of views that have been expressed by analysts of corporate performance. It is clear that they cannot be regarded in isolation, since many of the determinants or factors are bound to interact or overlap. As already mentioned, the technology and productivity hypotheses incorporate the same premises and affect each other (advances in technology help to improve productivity and higher productivity tends to stimulate the search for more effective technology), though their starting points and conclusions may not be identical. Similarly, technology and economies of scale interact: the introduction of new technology may not be feasible without the prospect of achieving a high sales volume, while companies cannot improve their competitiveness and expand their operations without the adoption of new technology.

In the same vein, the product and market theories have a great deal in common and listing them separately merely serves to emphasize the difference in managerial orientation: managers who believe in product dominance look for innovation first and then consider how to create a market for it, while those who hold with market dominance try first to ascertain what the market wants and then proceed to design and supply products that would satisfy the perceived market needs.

Thus, the dominant factor highlighted by each of the theories does not imply that all the other factors are ignored, or thought to be irrelevant, but indicates what their proponents believe to be most significant in the industrial scene. However, the alternative theories do not merely indicate differences in emphasis, but have profound consequences on internal allocation of resources and on the degree to which the relevant key functions in the organization influence overall strategy. Many case studies have been recorded to illustrate both the positive and negative effects of adhering too closely to one particular school.

For example, product dominance may be highlighted by the activities of an enthusiastic inventor, who has started with a new product that later became the foundation for a thriving large corporation. Had he not enjoyed the support of colleagues and financiers when that support was needed, the product would not have been developed in time to make the impact that it did on the market. On the other hand, there are equally persuasive examples of ingenious ideas that failed to generate adequate market response and eventually bled their companies to death. Similar examples can be cited with respect to each of the above determinants or factors. The adoption of any particular one as the prime ingredient of one's managerial philosophy is no guarantee of ultimate success.

A complex network of variables

Thus, it is important to note that none of these factors *on its own* may be regarded as a *necessary* explanation for various levels of financial success, but only as a *sufficient* condition. What this means is that when a particular premiss highlights a dominant attribute, X, it does not follow that one company must be superior to another with respect to X in order to be more successful. For example, when productivity is singled out as a key contributor to success, that does not imply that all successful companies are bound to have a better productivity record than their competitors; we may only surmise that if they are better with respect to productivity then they are *likely* to be more successful.

Furthermore, the weight of the evidence from case studies suggests that premises based on single dominant factors are far too simplistic. In reality, many variables interact through a complex web of relationships, which are not always amenable to explicit fomulation, so that changes in relative performance need to be attributed to a mix of variables. And since the mix itself varies enormously from one case study to another, definitive arguments for causal relationships are difficult to sustain.

A simple classification of the variables affecting corporate performance is suggested in the matrix in Table 3.1, characterized by

Table 3.1 Variables affecting corporate performance

	Quantitative	Qualitative
External	A	B
Internal	C	D

two dimensions. The first highlights the variables that are primarily outside the control of management, as opposed to those that are determined internally and are therefore affected by managerial decisions; the second distinguishes between variables that are measurable quantitatively and those that can only be described in qualitative terms. Thus, groups A and C in the matrix cover external and internal factors respectively and both sets can be measured quantitatively. Here are some examples pertaining to the four groups in the table:

Group A Interest rates, currency exchange rates, prices of raw materials, national wage agreements, tax rates.

Group B Competitors' image, militancy of trade unions, attitudes of governmental agencies.

Group C Product strategy (specification, variety, quality), resource allocation, pricing policy, employee incentive schemes.

Group D Organization structure, managerial style.

Clearly any modelling exercise that attempts to relate corporate performance to a given set of attributes must start with clear definitions of the attributes, which is where serious problems of measurement methodologies can arise. For some attributes, several alternative measures are possible and it is then necessary to determine which should be used. For example, company size may be measured by the sales volume in physical or revenue terms, by the value of its equity, by the total assets, by the number of employees, and so on. Other attributes are less amenable to measurement. For example, it is not at all clear how a methodology is to be designed to measure the degree to which a company is 'market-oriented', or 'leader-dominated'.

Perhaps it should be borne in mind that measurement in this context need not be confined to the construction of a continuous or even an ordinal scale, and that for the purpose of modelling corporate performance a simple classification represented by several discrete categories may also be helpful. For some attributes, which at first sight seem qualitative in nature, it may nevertheless be possible to devise direct or surrogate measures, as suggested by the following examples:

(a) The degree to which a company is dominated by such functions as production, marketing, R&D, or finance, may be assessed by the relative number of employees employed in each department, or by the relative size of departmental budgets.

(b) Indicators of organizational hierarchy may be given by the ratio of managerial personnel (appropriately defined) to the total number of employees in an organizational unit, or by the height of the hierarchical pyramid.

(c) Concern for R&D and innovation may be measured by company expenditure on these activities, or the proportion of R&D expenditure as a percentage of the total budget (in some companies there are ambiguities as to what activities come under the R&D umbrella and clearly they need to be carefully identified for the purpose).

(d) Product variety may be measured by the characteristics of the Pareto cumulative sales curve, which indicates what percentages of the product mix generate given percentages of the total revenue.

And so on. Naturally, all surrogate measures have their shortcomings, and when several measures are available, it becomes a matter of judgement (and convenience) as to which to choose. Any attempt to construct a measurement methodology helps to deepen our understanding of what we seek to measure, even if it does not immediately improve the prospect of constructing a definitive model of corporate performance.

This is why analysts persist in trying to convert qualitative attributes into quantitative ones. Some of the examples mentioned in conjunction with the above matrix may be cited to illustrate how ingenious yardsticks may be proposed as a result of market research studies or a variety of attitudinal questionnaires. It must be recognized, however, that there are limits to the scope of such exercises. Some attributes will always remain qualitative and descriptive in nature, so that the judgement, intuition and flair of experienced analysts will continue to have their place in making evaluations of the reasons for corporate success or failure.

Centralization v. decentralization

Arguments on the question of centralization v. decentralization highlight a further difficulty worthy of mention, namely that in constructing hypotheses in this field we are sometimes struck by the *duality syndrome*, namely by the fact that contradictory propositions may be advanced to explain a given phenomenon. A good example to illustrate this difficulty relates to the degree of centralization or decentralization in the organization of large companies.

This issue has been widely suggested as an important factor that affects corporate performance. The rationale for such a hypothesis goes something like this: Take a company that has many subsidiaries or branches (for example, several production facilities or distribution outlets). These subsidiaries or branches are in need of common supplies and services, such as raw materials, furniture, office supplies, word processors, computer terminals, travel facilities. Each subsidiary on its own can hardly hope to secure the level of discounts and promptness of delivery that a centralized purchasing office can exact from suppliers.

Similarly, various centralized functions relating to marketing, distribution, computing and management services, operational research, treasury management, legal services, and others, have the merit of pooling professional expertise at a lower cost than that which would be incurred if the subsidiaries or branches were left to fend for themselves. It may, therefore, be argued, that a company opting for a high degree of centralization will be in an advantageous position compared with one operating a decentralized structure.

On the other hand, a centralized organization deprives a subsidiary of freedom of action to make its own decisions. It is not allowed, for example, to choose a 'non-standard' computer terminal, to choose its own legal adviser, to seek alternative suppliers of stationery – because all these services are available centrally. While centralization is devised as a means of providing efficient services at reduced costs, it tends to stifle local initiative and distort local accountability. Similarly, when operational decision making is centralized, requiring decisions to be referred to the centre for approval before they can be implemented (for example, when the decisions involve capital expenditure, recruitment of senior managers, or commitments to customers), the main advantage is the attainment of a high degree of consistency in the quality of the decisions made.

The downside is, again, that local managers are deprived of authority and, because of its inherent hierarchical nature, the decision process can become rather long and cumbersome. In some cases, and particularly when the subsidiary is geographically remote from head office, the advantages of centralization can thereby be completely annulled. The balance between centralization and decentralization is closely related to the issue of accountability and demarcation of responsibility, which is further discussed in Chapter 8 entitled 'Divide and Rule'.

We see, therefore, how two perfectly plausible but contradictory hypotheses can be constructed, one stating that centralization must have a beneficial effect on corporate performance, the other suggesting the exact opposite. Which is right?

There does not seem to be definitive evidence to settle this question one way or the other. I am reminded of an example of two major hotel and restaurant chains, one with a highly centralized head office to incorporate many of the functions listed earlier, the other with a very small head office, confined to the financial control and treasury functions. The first was run by a charismatic father-figure committed to achieving uniform standards of service and performance throughout the network. The other was headed by a highly respected entrepreneur, who preferred to run his empire as a conglomerate, allowing each autonomous outlet to develop its own identity and its own managerial style. Admittedly, it would be impossible to argue that apart from their head offices the two chains were absolutely identical in terms of size, product range, customer base, or marketing strategies. However, the consensus among many informed observers was that the most blatant difference between the two enterprises was the degreee of centralization at the head office. The curious judgement of these observers was that both chains were regarded as very successful.

What conclusions can one draw from the two case studies? Admittedly, two cases constitute too small a sample for any definitive answer, but in the absence of other comparable companies in the industry, we are faced with several possible explanations:

(a) The possibility cannot be excluded that the good corporate performance in both cases was attributable to factors other than the question of centralization v. decentralization, and that this issue has no bearing on whether an enterprise operating in that industry and that economic environment is successful or not.

(b) The fact that both chains were successful does not mean that if either chose to emulate the head-office structure and operating procedures of the other, it would not become even more successful.

(c) Even if the adopted organizational mode does have an effect on success, neither is an 'optimal' way to organize the head office. It is conceivable that a different structure, for example a mixed mode which combined some aspects of centralization and some of decentralization, would have the benefits of both and would perform better than either.

It is far from clear which of these explanations is the most appropriate, and the limited sample size does not help. Even when studies in search of magic organizational formulae to guarantee corporate success are based on larger statistical samples, the conclusions are far from convincing. In the next chapter we discuss one such example, concerning the question of size of the board of directors and, as we shall see, the study raises more questions than it is able to resolve.

Conclusion: beware of exaggerated claims

All this suggests that in spite of persuasive arguments by specialists, acting as organization consultants and claiming to know 'the answer' to the difficult strategic issue of which determinants make an enterprise successful, one has to remain sceptical. The experience of these consultants, however vast, is necessarily confined to the particular case studies with which they have been involved, and from which it is doubtful that generalized theories can be inferred. Alas, the problem of identifying determinants of corporate perform-ance is immensely intricate and remains unresolved. The multitude of variables and attributes (some of which are qualitative in nature), the extraordinary difficulties in setting up measurement criteria, the bias inherent in selected surrogate measures – all these, coupled with the duality syndrome, explain why the vast case-study litera-ture has so far failed to produce a general corporate performance theory.

And as the socioeconomic environment continues to change, the body of knowledge accumulated by past case studies become less relevant for the analysis and comprehension of new case material. Perhaps we shall never have enough research evidence in terms of quantity and homogeneity to justify the construction of lasting hypotheses in this field. But those in search of theory will no doubt persist in their quest. The journey ahead remains long and tortuous, as ever.

CHAPTER 4

Board size and corporate failure

Board structure

In the previous chapter we discussed whether it is possible – with our current state of knowledge – to identify the major determinants of corporate performance. In particular, the following question was posed: 'Given two companies belonging to the same industrial sector and operating in the same environment, what makes one more successful than the other?' The practical implications of this question are self-evident, and it is therefore not surprising that students of business policy devote a great deal of time searching for relevant answers. The discussion in the previous chapter concluded that, however you define 'success' and whatever the lessons learnt from case studies and current research, the problem of identifying what factors determine a given level of corporate performance is still unresolved.

My interest was, therefore, greatly aroused when I came across a paper by Chaganti *et al.* (1985) on the effect of corporate board size on corporate failure. A great deal of attention has been devoted, by consultants and students of the managerial scene, to the problem of board structure and composition. As the board has the ultimate legal and moral responsibility for the welfare of the enterprise, it is obviously important to ensure that it is constituted in a way that would enhance its ability to carry out this responsibility effectively.

Three major questions regarding the board structure and operation then arise. The first relates to the composition of the board, including such issues as the necessary criteria for membership, the election process, and the means of striking a balance between the need for the board to act as a team with a unity of purpose in decision making and the need for individual members to retain their critical judgement and independence of mind, the number of 'outsiders' (non-executive directors) versus 'insiders', and the balance between the executive directors (namely, between those in charge of operating units as opposed to those responsible for staff and head-office functions). The second question concerns the way the board actually works, its procedures, the frequency of meetings, the range of topics tabled for discussion, and the degree of authority delegated to the board's standing and ad hoc committees.

Board size

The third question simply concerns the size of the board, and it is this issue that the paper by Chaganti *et al.* is primarily concerned with. The authors used the opportunity of their empirical research to address two subsidiary structural issues: the first involves the number of outsiders serving on the board and the second addresses the question of whether the fact that the CEO (Chief Executive Officer) does or does not hold another office in the organization (in addition to his responsibilities as CEO) has any bearing on the incidence of company failure.

Intuitively, size must influence the way that a board operates and the effectiveness with which discussions on major issues are conducted at board level. If the board consists only of a handful of individuals, it soon develops into a small exclusive clique which can become inward-looking, increasingly isolated from the rest of the organization and deprived of the opportunity to consider fresh and independent viewpoints.

On the other hand, issues requiring attention can be swiftly dealt with. If the board is too large, consisting of twenty or thirty individuals (some boards are even larger), it can soon become a talking shop and even minor issues then tend to take an inordinate amount of time to discuss. In large boards, a great deal of effort is needed just to keep all the members well informed by plying them with mounds of paperwork, and many important decisions get delayed and frustrated by increasing bureaucracy, so that the real power of policy formulation, let alone of decision and execution, tends to be performed by a policy or executive committee, which essentially operates as a board within a board.

Is there an optimal size for the board, and is the performance of the enterprise correspondingly affected? Apart from the obvious importance of the subject matter and its practical implications, the research methodology that might be employed to explore such an issue raises some intriguing questions, particularly since such a methodology, if it proves to be persuasive and flexible, could well be relevant for other research work in this area.

Success and failure

Instead of looking at industry at large and using 'corporate success' as a yardstick, with all the problems of definitions and measurement that such a concept would entail, Chaganti *et al.* chose to look at companies in the retailing industry in the USA that managed to survive. These are contrasted in their paper with companies that failed over a five-year period (failure being defined by the filing for bankruptcy under Chapter 11 of the Bankruptcy Act), so that in this context 'success' is simply epitomized by corporate survival, without trying to differentiate between different levels of 'success', and similarly there is no attempt in the study to distinguish between different degrees of failure. The question here, therefore, is whether the corporate board, in terms of its size and composition, can affect the probability of corporate survival.

The reasons for the authors' investigation stem from increasing pressures in recent years to reform corporate boards and to introduce legislation 'to assure desirable board governance'. It has been suggested that since the consequences of corporate failure can be very harmful and distressing to customers, employees, shareholders, banks, suppliers, and other sections of the community, corporate survival must be the prime objective of the board. Any legislation that can support the board in this objective would then be amply justified. It is in the light of such arguments that studies (as the one undertaken by the authors) may be helpful in providing useful guidelines.

The functions of the board

Chaganti *et al.* start by quoting the functions of corporate boards, as listed in a Conference Board Report in 1967, namely:

1 To establish broad policies and objectives
2 To appoint the senior executives, determine their terms of reference, approve their actions and monitor their performance
3 To safeguard and approve changes in corporate assets
4 To approve important financial decisions and to issue reports to the shareholders
5 To delegate powers to executives to act on behalf of the board
6 To maintain, enforce and revise as necessary the corporate charter
7 'To ensure the maintenance of a sound board'.

While the report which cites these functions was written quite some time ago, its description of the board's tasks would generally still be endorsed today, although perhaps greater emphasis would currently be put on concern for employees, on social responsibilities (which can take many forms), on business ethics, on concern for the environment, on disclosure of information, on the need to avoid conflicts of interest, and so on. In addition, one may query, with justification, the meaning of the seventh statement in the above list. What does the statement 'maintenance of a sound board' mean? Is it merely a general exhortation in support of motherhood, decency and civilized behaviour? And would it not be preferable to have more explicit definitions of responsibility and accountability?

It is generally agreed that ultimately it is the board's function to enhance the wellbeing of the enterprise by taking responsibility for the direction of operations and for monitoring performance, and it is not uncommon to find boards being criticized for corporate failings (for example, by financial analysts or by judges in the courts) in that respect. The questions posed by the authors regarding the possible effect of boards on corporate failure are, therefore, understandable.

Three propositions

The study examines three main propositions:

P1 *A non-failed firm tends to have a larger sized board than a failed firm.*

P2 *A non-failed firm tends to have a larger percentage of outsiders compared to a failed one. Somewhat along the same line, a non-failed firm tends to have a majority of outsiders; in contrast, a failed firm tends to have outsiders in the minority.*

P3 *In a non-failed firm, the chairman does not hold another office, like that of the CEO, in the company. In contrast, in a failed firm the chairman holds at least one other office.*

The first proposition is solely concerned with size, simply suggesting that the larger the board the better; the second addresses the question of the proportion of outside directors, and the third is concerned with whether the fact that the chairman holds another ofice in the organization or not has an effect on corporate failure.

The methodology

As a research methodology, the authors selected 42 boards of retailing firms, half of which had failed between 1970 and 1976 (retailing constituted the largest segment of commercial and business failures in the USA at that time). Each failed firm in the sample was paired with a non-failed one of a similar type and comparable size, and the differences in board size and structure in each pair were noted for a period of five years prior to the failure of each failed firm. In this way, the investigators tried to ensure that the firms in each pair were subjected to similar economic and social conditions.

Now, although the set of firms used in this investigation had been used in other published studies, and although 'comparability of the firms in each pair has been tested and goodness of the set for use in paired design has generally been acknowledged' (Chaganti *et al.* 1985: 409–10), I confess to feeling somewhat uncomfortable with this methodology. Since a large number of firms in the industry have not failed, it is presumably possible in most cases to pair a failed firm with any one from a set of many non-failed firms of similar type and size, and since the non-failed firms are likely to differ widely in the size and structure of their boards, the selection process in this paired design may well be crucial and may significantly affect the conclusions to be drawn from the investigation.

Suppose, for example, that the selected non-failed firm has the average board size of all the non-failed firms in its set, and suppose that this average is higher than that of the failed firm in the pair. This result would seem to support proposition *P1*, but if a significant proportion of the firms in the non-failed set have a smaller board size than the failed firm, can this fact be ignored in making a judgement about *P1*? Similarly, if the non-failed firm is selected at random and if its board size is larger than the average board size of the set of non-failed firms, is it justifiable to ignore the firms with smaller boards than the failed firm in drawing conclusions from this research? To what extent, therefore, are conclusions derived from studies based on such paired comparisons sensitive to the sample size of available data and to the choice of the pairs?

The results

Leaving aside these crucial problems of the research methodology, let us turn to the authors' findings. The justification for the level of detail given here lies with the need to point out how alert one must be in assessing and accepting the relevance of 'researched results'.

First, with reference to proposition *P2*, the results showed that over the five-year period considered in the study, the percentage of outside directors on the boards of failed firms ranged from 17 to 86, compared with 20 to 80 in the non-failed firms. Clearly, both ranges are very wide, with a marked degree of overlap. Also, the average of outsiders for the failed group was 51%, compared with 49.6% for the non-failed. These results (and other considerations which are not elaborated here) rightly led the authors to reject proposition *P2*. Similarly, the results showed that the chairman held at least another office in 7–10 failed firms, compared with 9–11 non-failed firms, and furthermore the differences across the pairs were not significant, so that proposition *P3* was also rejected.

This leaves proposition *P1*, which the authors assert is confirmed by their study. They claim that their first proposition 'suggests that the non-failed firms, as compared to the failed firms, tend to have larger boards', and 'that this observation was further confirmed by the pair-wise t-test at 95% confidence level' (Chaganti *et al.* 1985: 411). Reference to their table of data reveals a very wide overlap between the ranges of board size of failed and non-failed firms, so that yet again one needs to ask whether the results of the statistical tests are not sensitive to the sample size and to the paired design.

But even if the statistical results of this study were sufficiently convincing, what possible lessons can be drawn from it in normative terms? If we are entitled to infer from proposition *P1* that having a larger board reduces the probability of corporate failure, then we need to ask: larger than what? Should it be larger than the average size of boards of failed companies, or larger than the largest of all the recorded failed companies in the industrial sector? Does proposition *P1* imply that the larger the size the better for corporate survival? Would a board of a hundred directors, or two hundred (or more?), immunize the company from failure? Any such inferences would clearly be absurd.

Cause and effect

Thus, even if we assume that proposition *P1* is not refuted by contradicting empirical evidence, we have to conclude that no practical inferences can be drawn from such a study. It should be realized that the proposition merely points to an association of two characteristics (one being an average of a widely distributed variable and the other representing the binary state of failure or non-failure), but provides no causal relationship between them.

There is nothing in the study that suggests that firms failed *because* they had small boards, and that, had they taken action in good time to increase the size of their boards, all their problems would have been resolved. Apart from the fact that such a causal relationship would be quite impossible to establish in a research exercise of this kind, there is always the distinct possibility that the size of the board is merely a manifestation of other factors which influence the operations of the company and the level of its performance, rather than board size per se being the primary cause. It is quite likely that if a chairman, instead of addressing himself to the root causes of poor performance of his company, decides on the simple-minded remedy of increasing the size of his board, he would eventually find that such an act of faith has done little to extricate the company from its difficulties.

Conclusion

The research work discussed here is an example of the wide range of investigations that propositions on corporate performance, such as the one discussed in this chapter or the various hypotheses outlined in the previous chapter, can be embarked upon. I chose this example not because of its intrinsic importance or because of its earth-shattering results, but because – like many other studies of its kind – it culminates with the claim of establishing an association between two variables (in this case between board size and corporate failure) with the implication of causality. In view of the multitude of variables that affect industrial phenomena, and the difficulties encountered in reality in collecting unbiased data, coupled with the impossibility of engaging in experimental design, the desire to reduce complex functional linkages into a simple relationship which relies only on two variables is understandably beguiling. This is why the research methodology employed in all investigations of this kind requires close scrutiny.

The motives that led Chaganti *et al.* to undertake this research are laudable enough. If boards are supposed to have an effect on the welfare of their firms, it is natural to probe into the circumstances under which they succeed or fail. My scepticism about the value of such research, though, stems not only from doubts about the validity of the research methodology, but from the distinct possibility that, at most, what has been established is an *association* between the two variables, not *causality*. The danger is that when association is interpreted as causality, it can lead to the creation of simple-minded mechanistic recipes, examples of which have become so fashionable and so captivating on the managerial scene in recent years; alas, many of the recipes have not lived up to their promise and had eventually to be abandoned.

One cannot help the feeling that searches for single determinants of corporate performance are more than likely to be abortive. There are many factors that help or hinder corporate excellence, but board size seems hardly relevant in this context. As the authors observe, a small board can be more easily 'managed' by the CEO, but then its members may not have adequate opportunities to influence policy and operations, whereas a large board can offer a wider range of expertise, but may be more difficult to control and can become bogged down by procedural inactivity. It is not at all obvious which of these attributes are more conducive to the achievement of corporate goals, as much depends on the style of management of the CEO, not to mention the mix of personalities of his (or her) colleagues on the board.

It is, therefore, not the size of the board that matters, but many other issues associated with it, such as:

- how it operates,
- the quality of the information at its disposal,
- the way in which it gets involved in setting objectives and budgets,
- the kind of decisions it takes, and
- the way it exercises control over the executive directors of the company.

These issues are probably far more significant in ensuring that the board does direct the affairs of the enterprise and controls its effectiveness, but these issues are less amenable to a simple statistical analysis of the kind reported by Chaganti *et al.*

References

Chaganti, R. S., Mahajan, V. and Sharma, S. 1985. Corporate boardsize, composition and corporate failures in retailing industy. *International Management Studies* 22 (4), 400–17.

Conference Board 1967. Corporate directorship practices, studies in business policy. New York: Conference Board.

CHAPTER 5

OR at the top?

Need for a think-tank

As suggested in Chapter 1, the chaotic environment in which business and industry have to operate has encouraged theorists and practitioners in the managerial arena to seek ways in which unstructured problems can be structured, so that decision making can be guided by systematic procedures and consistency. This search for a rationale, or what some academics call 'a theory of management', is an attempt to examine the operation of business systems and to understand the reasons for changes in their behaviour and performance.

In many ways this search is akin to scientific inquiries relating to the behaviour of systems in the natural world. Several thousand years ago, man was bewildered by the seemingly chaotic characteristics of many physical phenomena, but the history of science is a testimony of how, bit by bit, Nature has yielded some of its secrets in response to the probing of dedicated scientists. It is tempting to suggest that a systematic scientific inquiry into the nature of the business world would reveal a set of basic laws, similar to the laws of Nature, and that these would provide the rationale for managing and controlling industrial and business enterprises.

There are, of course, many fundamental differences between the physical world and the business world. Perhaps the most important difference is that the physical world is perceived as being governed by a set of orderly physical laws, so that scientists can study essentially the same systems or phenomena over many decades or even centuries, and the validity of past data is not eroded just because of the passage of time. Also, many phenomena are of relatively short duration and can be observed repeatedly, often by the same investigator, and masses of data can be collected, scrutinized, compared with past observations, and form the basis for hypothesis testing.

Where phenomena are subject to trends or long cyclical variations, as in the fields of climatology and astronomy, the observations of generations of investigators are painstakingly put together to form patterns and trends that help to unravel the mysteries of Nature. In some areas, such as toxicological studies, investigations into the effects of different types of food on health, or research on the consequences of pollution on the environment, the systems under observation are themselves subject to change and the statistical nature of the cause-and-effect relationships make the conduct of scientific inquiry much more difficult and inevitably time-consuming. However, past observations continue to form an important part of the data bank for a total scientific inquiry.

By contrast, the business arena is highly volatile, is greatly affected by human behaviour (a domain which itself is random and often unpredictable) and is subject to discrete and abrupt changes over relatively short time horizons. This volatility, coupled with the complex relationships between numerous variables, as mentioned in Chapter 1, compounds the difficulties of systematic observations and data-collection exercises; consequently, progress towards creating a rationale and a theory of management is bound to be painfully slow.

Nevertheless, many believe that the application of the scientific method is the only hope of making any headway in the acquisition of knowledge and a better understanding of the business world. Senior executives live in a dynamic industrial environment and are under constant pressure to react to ever changing circumstances. Furthermore, the rate of change has accelerated in recent years, partly due to impact of technology and innovation in general and information technology in particular, and partly due to significant changes in the market-place and the realignments of powerful industrial blocs, leading to keener competition at home and the opening of new markets abroad.

When one considers that the CEO constantly has to face myriads of issues of varying complexity and has to make decisions under great pressure, often with little time to indulge in a detailed investigation of alternatives and possible outcomes, one would expect that help at various stages of the decision process would be essential. What the CEO needs is a kind of think-tank to help analyse changing circumstances, examine new threats and opportunities, and formulate appropriate responses to these challenges.

Since the Second World War it has been strongly suggested that OR (operational research) could fill this role of a think-tank at the commanding heights of an industrial organization. This hope was based on the experience of OR during the war, when scientists were called upon to advise senior military commanders and politicians on the conduct of operations, and it was natural to assume that after the war an analogous service could be provided in the world of business. Has this expectation been matched by reality?

The reality

A great deal has been written about the fact that – in spite of its great potential and promise – OR has not managed to find a suitable role in the corridors of power in industry and commerce and that, on the whole, it has failed to make an indelible impact on decision processes right at the top of the managerial hierarchy. There are, of course, many examples where the OR contribution has been absolutely indispensable to the formulation of strategy and where CEOs have been lavish in their praise of the OR activity in their organizations, but such examples are relatively rare.

For the most part, the OR group reports at such a low level in the organizational structure (see, for example, Eilon 1985), that the CEO has only a vague notion, if any, of what his OR people are up to. And indeed, for the most part there is no reason for him (or her) to be so informed, since much of the OR work is confined to technical and tactical problems that do not concern the CEO at all. The question, therefore, remains: why has OR usually been conspicuous by its absence at the strategic level? In seeking to gain a better understanding of this question, it may be instructive to look at it from the viewpoint of those who occupy positions at the senior echelons of their organizations and to highlight certain characteristics of the problems facing them.

Objectives and aspirations at the top

First, let us look at objectives at the top level of the organization. As indicated in earlier chapters, discussions with senior executives tend to reveal that it is rare for these objectives to be described by a single criterion. Many criteria are at play, some defined explicitly, others 'emerge' when alternative courses of action are contemplated. The problem for the analyst is that a multi-objective formulation does not help in ranking alternative strategies. However, trade-offs between objectives are often not specified, so that attempts to reduce a multi-objective system to a single criterion (which is what most OR analysts are comfortable with), in order to help the decision-making process, become controversial and raise questions of validity.

Furthermore, the objectives are not always stated in clear quantitative terms, and the means by which they are measured are ill defined, or subject to alternative interpretations, so that arguments may well arise as to whether, in a particular situation, a given objective has in fact been achieved or not. In some cases, senior executives are reluctant, or feel unable, to formulate their objectives, and the lack of clear definitions leads to ambiguities about what the objectives really are. Pressed about what he was trying to achieve, one CEO responded: 'I cannot describe it in advance, but I'll recognize it when I see it'. This genuine inability to specify objectives is by no means uncommon. The many aspects of objectives at the top level of the managerial hierarchy are summarized in Table 5.1.

We also need to realize that the objectives of the organization are not necessarily identical to those of the individuals at the top, in terms of their own personal aspirations or the needs of their departments (or subsidiaries). Such a conflict may well affect the whole process of determining corporate objectives, when the same key individuals are involved. This is one of the reasons for the existence of a 'hidden agenda' at the top level of the organization: the declared objectives are not always what they seem, and a great deal of spade-work is required to uncover their 'true' meaning.

Inability or reluctance to specify objectives often manifests itself by ambivalence about constraints, which essentially define the boundaries within which strategies and courses of action need to be

Table 5.1 Objectives at the top level

- Multi-criterion
  - * for the organization as a whole
  - * for various interested parties
- Ambiguity ('I'll recognize it when I see it')
- Hidden agenda
- Inability (often) to specify criteria
- Ambivalence about constraints
- Short term versus long term
- Incoherent hierarchy
  - * difficulties in disaggregation
  - * sub-objectives may be incompatible
  - * conflict with personal goals
- Satisficing instead of optimizing

ascertained. Leaving aside external constraints (dictated by legal or regulatory authorities, national and international agreements, trading practices, currency exchange rates, and so on), managers often cite a host of internal constraints that limit their authority and their room for manoeuvre. These constraints, which are imposed by the organization in order to delineate procedures and enforce accountability, are part of a managerial control system, helping every echelon in the structure to keep track of what goes on at lower levels (this is further discussed in Chapter 13).

Two observations need to be made about internal constraints. The first is that, as discussed elsewhere (Eilon 1979a), many of these constraints are essentially no different from objectives; for example, whether achieving a pre-specified desirable level of return on investment is considered to be a constraint ('determine an operating plan, subject to the constraint that return on investment does not fall below level X') or an objective ('determine an operating plan that will yield a return on investment of at least X') is more a matter of semantics than substance. Secondly, the lower you go in the organizational pyramid, the more closely defined the internal constraints are, becoming almost part of an elaborate code of operational discipline, and conversely, the higher you go, the less stringent is their definition and the more ambivalence is encountered as to whether the constraints should be rigidly and mechanistically adhered to (Eilon 1979b).

Another serious problem about objectives is the conflict between the short term and the long term. It has often been said that any fool can improve the financial performance of an industrial enterprise by drastic cost-cutting measures, such as the elimination of R&D, cancellation of the design of new products, postponement of all capital expenditure projects, suspension of graduate recruitment, and so on. The short-term effects of such actions may well be quite dramatic, but to the detriment and at the expense of corporate performance in the long term, as further discussed in Chapter 6. Senior executives are well aware of this conflict, and the balance that they seek to strike between the two is inevitably affected by the day-to-day pressures under which the organization has to operate, as well as by the perceived consequences for the individuals concerned.

There also exists an incoherent hierarchy of objectives throughout the organizational structure. This is caused by difficulties in disaggregating objectives set at the top into clear and compatible sub-objectives at lower levels, by the conflict that often arises between various parts of the organization competing for recognition and rewards that come with success, as well as by the conflict alluded to earlier between organizational and personal goals.

But perhaps the most important feature about objectives at the top level is the last item listed in Table 5.1, following the observation made by Simon many years ago (and echoed by many others), namely that senior executives are more attuned to thinking in terms of satisficing, rather than optimizing. Satisficing is the philosophy of selecting a solution that 'is good enough', whereas optimizing seeks to find the best solution according to some pre-specified criterion. OR analysts have tried to cope with this phenomenon by introducing goal-programming models, which have been extensively regurgitated in the literature, though their applicability in most situations is a matter of some doubt (Eilon 1979a).

Strategic decisions

And there is more. Apart from the fundamental problems encountered by OR analysts in trying to ascertain what objectives senior executives aim for (as listed in Table 5.1), there are many other

Table 5.2 Other problems for strategic decision making

- Incomplete information
- New ventures (no track record)
- Imprecise decision nodes
- Consequences of delayed decisions
- Unquantified risk
- External threats

  * competition
  * new products and technology
  * changes in rules and regulations
  * take-over and loss of independence

- Evolution versus revolution
- Difficulties in measurement of:

  * inputs
  * outputs or outcomes
  * performance

- Long response times

  * inherent in the industry
  * organizational inertia

---

issues that affect decision making at the strategic level, and some are summarized in Table 5.2. First, it must be recognized that strategic decisions are rarely made with complete information. Senior executives often feel that they would need more information before committing vast resources to a new venture, or before they decide to abandon certain activities and embark on a new direction, and the prime purpose of seeking additional information is to reduce the degree of risk that may be involved.

However, more information may not be available, or may be too costly and very time-consuming to gather. Furthermore, if deliberations relate to a new venture (involving a new product, a new market, the adoption of new technology, large investment in R&D), there is no proven track record that can be relied upon in an evaluation of future performance, so that conventional modelling exercises are only as convincing as the assumptions on which they are based.

A strategic decision rarely involves a single event, and the 'final' decision of whether to proceed with a particular venture is always the culmination of a long process of planning, weighing up alternatives, discarding certain proposals and introducing new ones, adjusting and refining. A major difficulty for the analyst is that he (she) often encounters a network of imprecise decision nodes, in that it is not always clear who makes the intermediate decisions that shape the final proposals, nor is it clear when they are made. An understanding of this fuzzy network is essential for those wishing to influence the decision process, but is often very difficult to come by.

This elaborate strategic decision process is based on the realization that far-reaching consequences for the future welfare of the organization may be at stake. This is why managers are loath to take unnecessary risks, and (as already stated above) one way for them to reduce risk is to seek more information, which in turn delays the final decision. What complicates the process even further is that, in addition to the explicit consequences of making decisions, there are also consequences resulting from delays, or from not making decisions at all, and that irrespective of the amount of effort that is invested in gathering more information, a certain level of unquantifiable and even unidentifiable risk always remains.

External threats

Another problem for strategic decision makers, also highlighted in Table 5.2, is the constantly looming array of external threats: threats from current competitors as well as from newcomers, threats to the existing product range and methods of manufacture from new products and new technology, threats from changing rules and regulations regarding production and trading practices, and threats from a possible take-over with the resultant loss of independence for the company and even loss of office for the senior executives. All these threats often have a direct or an indirect effect on the strategic decision process and on corporate objectives.

Against this constant background of external threats and risks, the top management needs to determine whether to progress cautiously by evolution, or to opt for drastic changes in the ethos of the organization and the scope of its operations. The choice between evolution and revolution is being faced by senior executives in one industry after another, and some find it a difficult choice to make. Most managers are a conservative lot and are more comfortable with an evolutionary process. For one thing, it allows more time for reassessment and readjustment to changing circumstances and reduces the risk of catastrophic outcomes, whereas most revolutionary changes are irreversible, involve many uncertainties and can get out of control.

But the choice is not merely a reflection of personal preferences for risk taking or risk aversion, although the psychological make-up of the senior executives involved undoubtedly plays a part; it is often forcibly brought about by the external pressures mentioned above, and in times of crisis even the most timid and introverted executive may decide that a revolutionary change is called for.

Modelling and measurement

All these problems, listed in Tables 5.1 and 5.2, amply demonstrate the difficulties facing OR analysts in their efforts to construct models for strategic decision making. Unlike the relatively clear-cut OR modelling exercises found in textbooks (and sometimes encountered in reality at the tactical level), decision making at the top is a messy business, cast against a background of incoherent objectives, ambiguous constraints and unspecified agenda. These are not features, even if they are clearly understood, that are amenable to be incorporated into a crisp decision model.

But as if all these issues were not enough, there are two further problems enumerated in Table 5.2 that need to be mentioned. The first is the difficulty of measurement: measurement of inputs, measurement of outputs and outcomes, and measurement of performance. This is not the place to elaborate on these topics, which are well documented in the literature (see, for example, Eilon 1984), but clearly they are crucial both for the decision process itself, and for the evaluation of its results.

The other problem is that strategic decisions often involve long response times, some are inherent in the industry (for example, large construction projects which may span several years), some are embedded in organizational inertia (particularly when a large and complex organization structure is involved), so that the senior executives who take the final decisions to implement change are not necessarily going to be there to witness the results. These factors, too, have an inevitable influence on the way in which the strategic decision problems are formulated and tackled.

Against the wide range of problems listed in Tables 5.1 and 5.2, let us now consider the typical profile of an OR analyst in industry, as shown in Table 5.3. I hasten to add that this description does not fit all OR analysts, and exceptions can no doubt be cited (particularly among OR managers). But the *typical* analyst is relatively young (a large majority of OR workers in industry are under 30) with limited managerial experience and limited knowledge of the industry. He (or she) is probably a graduate in OR (often with a degree in mathematics or statistics), and by the very nature of his background and education looks for highly structured problems, using quantitative modelling techniques that yield optimal solutions to problems, preferably with a single objective.

The consequences of such a profile are only to be expected (Table 5.3). The OR analyst tends to have a fairly narrow orientation, his obsession with quantitative modelling requires 'hard' data to feed into his models, and he therefore tends to concentrate on current operations for which reliable information can be obtained, rather than get involved with new ventures of a strategic nature, for which hard information is scanty. The result is that OR tends to be

Table 5.3 Typical profile of an OR analyst

- Relatively young
- Little managerial experience
- Limited knowledge of the industry
- Graduate in OR (often mathematics/statistics)
- Seeks highly structured problems
- Keen on quantitative modelling
- Looks for optimal solutions

Hence:

- narrow orientation
- 'analysis requires data'
- study of current operations
- reporting to middle management
- limited contact with top management

Result: *OR tends to focus on tactical problems and its successes serve to reinforce this position*

concerned with tactical problems and reports to middle management, so that its contacts with top management and strategic problems become rather limited.

When Table 5.3 is contrasted with Tables 5.1 and 5.2, we have an explanation for the absence of OR influence at the top. The make-up, the background and the aspirations of most OR analysts are not in tune with the messy and unstructured environment that prevails at the strategic decision-making level. But, as argued earlier, the need for advice and assistance at the top level remains. If one were to provide a description of the characteristics that would be needed for an OR support function at the top level of the organization, it would probably be as summarized by Table 5.4.

Table 5.4   Prerequisites for 'OR at the top'

- Good knowledge of the operations
- Confidence of the CEO
- Reporting at a director level
- Counselling skills

  * working 'with', not 'for'
  * reliability
  * objectivity
  * wisdom
  * maturity
  * ability to communicate

- Taking initiatives (being pro-active)
- Good reputation in the organization

The first prerequisite is that OR should have good knowledge of the operations and activities of the company, that the OR manager should enjoy the confidence of the CEO, and that he (she) should report at director level. The OR group should work 'with' (not 'for') senior executives in the organization and possess the appropriate counselling skills required for the purpose: reliabilty, objectivity, wisdom, maturity, and ability to communicate and share ideas with the executives. The OR people should not just sit passively in their cosy offices and wait for problems to be presented to them, but go out and look for new areas to study and new ventures to consider. OR at that level should be expected to take initiatives; in short, it should not be passive but be distinctly pro-active.

A possible solution

As most conventional OR groups are incapable of fulfilling this role, the question is: who should undertake it? Some CEOs call in external consultants to act as their strategy advisers and counsellors, who may bring their own teams of analysts and corporate planners. Others may resort to setting up a small group specifically designated as an internal think-tank, in effect a second OR group (whether it is called by that name or not), predominantly (but not exclusively) staffed by mature OR personnel with the kind of attributes listed in Table 5.4 and who are eager to operate at the strategic level. This would be a natural way to meet the needs of management at that level, but whether the creation of two OR groups, one dedicated to tactical problems and the other to strategy, can work in harmony in the same organization is another matter.

References

Eilon, S. 1979a. *Aspects of Management.* Oxford: Pergamon Press.
Eilon, S. 1979b. *Management Control.* Oxford: Pergamon Press.
Eilon, S. 1984. *The Art of Reckoning, Analysis of Performance Criteria.* London: Academic Press.
Eilon, S. 1985. *Management Assertions and Aversions.* Oxford: Pergamon Press.

CHAPTER 6

A simple formula

Performance expectations

The other day, I was talking to a senior manager of a large company about its corporate performance. The company had a highly structured reporting system, where every month a wide range of performance measures were assembled for the scrutiny of all the senior managers in the organization. We were in the fourth month of the new financial year and my friend and I were discussing the extent to which performance fell short of the expectations, as promulgated by the Board of Directors in the widely publicized corporate plan only a few months earlier. I was wondering about the possible reasons for the deviation from the budget and was about to embark on a detailed analysis of the figures.

But it soon became clear that, as my friend put it, he was 'not interested in a diagnosis but in action'. He pushed across his desk an internal memo from the CEO (Chief Executive Officer), addressed to all those in charge of cost and profit centres, pointing out that the quarterly results showed a serious shortfall in profit, compared with the target specified in the budget, and stating that if the quarterly figures were extrapolated to the end of the financial year, the outcome would be very embarrassing for all concerned.

On the advice of the corporate financial controller, the CEO concluded that a drastic cost-cutting exercise was urgently needed, with the aim of reducing the total cost for the remaining financial year by £20m. He proceeded to allocate this figure to the various operating units in proportion to their annual budgets, so that in percentage terms they would all be faced with the same cut. To help managers implement the cut, a firm of management consultants was engaged to undertake a detailed O&M (organization and methods) study of all the operations, as well as their corresponding manning levels, and produce a plan of action within three months.

The fire-fighting mentality

The CEO was clearly not going to allow matters to drift and get out of control, and he was resolved to do something about it. It is the kind of reaction that we have come to expect from senior executives, and indeed we have all seen it happen so often in large organizations. As outside observers or analysts, we are expected to sit back and admire the incisiveness demonstrated by these actions and speculate on the sophisticated analysis that may have preceded them, whereas in reality they are often devoid of any analysis and merely reflect short-term expediency.

It has been shown time and time again that short-term cost cutting is not very difficult to achieve. You start by cutting R&D, then training, then travelling, advertising and entertainment, even telephone calls during periods that involve peak rates; you then proceed to postpone all or most of the capital expenditure planned for the next few months, you postpone payments of all incoming invoices and pressurize your suppliers for additional discounts (on top of those already agreed when orders were generated) under the threat of switching your business to the competitors – in short you scrutinize every single item in the projected negative cash flow for the remainder of the financial year and seek ways to reduce it or eliminate it altogether.

In principle, this is the kind of exercise that was undertaken at the time of drafting the annual budget, but now – under the pressure and insistence of the CEO to cut costs by a specified amount, come what may – further avenues for reducing expenditure can be found. When all the projected measures are put into operation, you soon realize that indeed substantial cost savings can quickly be achieved, only to result in serious consequences in the long term.

Examples of consequences

Many examples can be cited to illustrate such consequences. One popular area for cost cutting, which has an immediate effect on cash flow, is that of recruitment. I have often come across a company that stopped recruiting university graduates altogether for a while, in order to save large sums of money on their induction training. Apart from an almost instantaneous impact on costs, there is usually no noticeable effect on immediate operational performance; in fact, the suspension of recruitment relieves managers and supervisors from the need to guide and look after the new recruits, and this enables them to attend to their many other duties and improve their day-to-day performance.

It does not take very long, though, before the company experiences difficulties in filling junior managerial vacancies and realizes that if the stoppage in a graduate input is allowed to continue, it would soon create a serious imbalance in the age and career profile at the lower end of the managerial structure, leading to depletion of potential managerial talent in years to come. Consequently, the company rushes to reverse its recruiting policy and attempts to redress the shortfall by increasing the intake of new graduates, even by trying to entice junior managers from other companies to join. As a result of this stop–go recruiting policy, the effect of the disruption stays with the organization for a long while and the costs incurred greatly exceed the original savings.

Another common example is that of training. Most enterprises realize that well-trained manpower is their most important asset and that it should therefore be nurtured and constantly improved. Each company then proceeds to invest in training with three objectives in mind: first, to ensure that its employees are well versed with internal systems and procedures; secondly, to improve the technical skills of the employees in performing their day-to-day tasks; and thirdly, to widen the knowledge base of employees and prepare them for future promotion and added responsibilities.

Suspension of all training programmes (and particularly those aimed at achieving the third objective) usually has only a minimal effect on the immediate efficiency with which operations are conducted, so that there is an understandable temptation to engage in short-term cost savings in that area. In this way, the manager in charge of an operating unit can defer expenditure on new personnel and on their training until the need for additional manpower becomes absolutely necessary, at which time recruitment can proceed either in the open market or by poaching from another part of the organization. Training the new recruits would then have been borne by others and not charged to the manager's budget, though the training costs for the company as a whole may not be alleviated.

Virtually all the examples that fall into the category of investment for the future – whether it is in modernizing facilities, in seeking to develop new products, or in creating a highly skilled workforce – have a common philosophy and purpose, namely that the investment today, which admittedly causes a negative cash flow, is intended to improve corporate operations tomorrow. The absence of this investment can only lead, in due course, to a deterioration in corporate performance. This serious problem, generally referred to as the philosophy of short-termism, is discussed further in the next chapter, and we return to certain organizational consequences of it in Chapter 13.

The ill-conceived doctrine of common misery

It is for these reasons that one must be dubious about the advisability and effectiveness of short-term cost-cutting exercises, particularly when they are imposed evenly across the board (i.e. in proportion to budgets), the so-called 'doctrine of common misery'. A much more sensible approach would be to relate cost to effectiveness, for example, the cost of individual operating units to their respective profit streams, so that cuts (if they have to be made) are selective and guided by the effect that they would have in each case.

After all, operating units in an enterprise are bound to operate unevenly and it is quite conceivable that some perform so well, and are potentially able to do even better, that their budgets should in fact be increased rather than cut! An evenly distributed cost-cutting dictum is, admittedly, much easier to 'sell' to an embattled managerial hierarchy and is likely to result in less bickering and animosity than a selective and uneven cost-cutting imposition. But the latter would make much more sense and would be more effective, if an honest and dispassionate analysis of performance is undertaken. A narrow and superficial view of a managerial problem in search of a 'quick fix' can easily lead to a short-term respite of questionable validity.

Alternative perceptions

The problem of balancing short-term considerations against long-term consequences is one of the most crucial issues facing senior management in the analysis of corporate strategy, as we shall see further in several chapters of this book. This balance is constantly under pressure when expected or promised performance measures are not met, and it is not difficult in every instance to prescribe remedies to relieve the pressure in the short term. The problem is that short-term relief does not constitute a cure, and very often makes the prospect of a cure more difficult and even remote.

This dichotomy is embedded in the different perceptions that managers have of the problems that they encounter, and the different perceptions lead to different notions of how they should be tackled. I am reminded of the story of the two sales managers of two competing shoe manufacturers, who were sent on a mission to explore the market in one of the corners of darkest Africa. They both went to the same places, read the same local newspapers, interviewed a sample of shopkeepers and inhabitants – in short, they conducted their market research in accordance with the 'infallible' principles they had learnt in their in-company training courses. When they came back, one reported to his boss that there was no market in that part of the world: most of the population walked barefoot and demand was bound to be very low. The other reported that as most of the population did not have any shoes, the potential market was huge and just waiting to be developed.

It is an old story, but it has an interesting message. In management, as in other areas of human endeavour, any given issue can be looked at and analysed from different viewpoints, leading to different conclusions and hence to different decisions and outcomes. Evaluation and action hinge on what is assumed as 'given' and what is regarded as a 'decision variable'. In other words, attitudes to problems and approaches to resolving them are largely governed by the definition of constraints, as well as by prevailing myths and taboos. These factors are so central to our understanding of the environment in which we operate, that they pervade the whole managerial process, from problem formulation, to modelling, to weighing alternative strategies, to decision and implementation. Furthermore, they very often determine management philosophy and style.

Perception of profit

To illustrate this point, let us examine three different outlooks that can be developed from the examination of the following very simple formula:

$$Profit = Revenue - Cost$$

Revenue is the total amount of money obtained from selling products and services, while the total cost is the monetary value of employing various resources to produce and supply these products and services. As the formula indicates, profit is defined as the difference between the two figures, so that it may be regarded as the outcome of two self-contained and often independent processes: the first is the process of making things, namely of converting material and labour inputs into products, and the effort expended in this process is represented by the total cost; the second is the process of selling these products, namely of converting them into money, and this is represented by the revenue.

The residual amount from these separate processes is profit, and since it is derived as the difference between two relatively large numbers, which are often variable and subject to fluctuations, it tends to be highly volatile and often strictly unpredictable. This can become a serious problem when the company's financial results are due to be published, putting the onus on management to consider ways of controlling the highly variable outcome. Consequently, we often find that management resorts to two separate actions aimed at 'managing' the final profit figure, in order to ensure that the declared profit figure is in accord with corporate objectives and market expectations:

- The first action is taken well before the final results are known and is aimed at influencing the two processes before the resultant profit is ascertained. The sales department is urged to maximize revenue, while the production department is pressurized to minimize costs, and various financial incentives are dangled in front of the employees to improve performance in these respects. The result may well be an increase in the expected value of profit compared with what would have transpired had no managerial cajoling taken place, but the inherent volatility of the outcome (being the difference between two relatively large numbers) remains.

- The second action is taken at the end of the period for which the accounts are to be released, when management analyses the results and decides that the profit is too low and is likely to disappoint the financial market, or that it is too high and could lead to unrealistic expectations in the following year. Management then proceeds to 'massage' the figures, for example, by assigning some cost or revenue items to the next financial period, in order to smooth the stream of profit and expenditure figures, and thereby project to the outside world (and particularly to the shareholders and financial analysts) an image of unruffled solidity.

Perception of revenue

Now consider the following variation of the same formula:

$$\text{Revenue} = \text{Cost} + \text{Profit}$$

In algebraic terms, this formula is identical to the one stated earlier, but psychologically it is very different. Here revenue is identified as the outcome of whatever cost and profit levels are obtained. The cost can be inferred from past performance and budget projections, thereby providing the basis for estimating the unit cost, which – for managerial purposes – is assumed to be 'given'. Management then specifies the level of the profit margin that would be acceptable to the board and to the market-place in comparison with competitors and the industry as a whole. The profit margin and the unit cost provide the basis for calculating the unit profit.

The formula then tells management what revenue, or a combination of unit price and volume, would be required in order to accommodate the estimated cost and to achieve the profit margin. Thus, the formula encapsulates the *cost-plus* mentality that is commonly encountered in some industries. Here, cost and profit are regarded as 'given', while the company's pricing policy is the so-called decision variable, the consequence of which is the revenue. In reality, of course, further assumptions need to be made about the effect of price on volume, but in many cost-plus situations the volume is determined by factors other than price, or is insensitive to it.

Perception of cost

The third variation of the same formula is given by:

$$\text{Cost} = \text{Revenue} - \text{Profit}$$

Again, the algebraic reformulation of this relationship is trivial, but the effect on managerial attitude is far-reaching. What the formula now says is that cost is the outcome of achieving certain levels of revenue and profit.

Here management starts with the market-place. What is the prevailing price in the market for the product that the company wishes to sell? What are the pricing policies of the competitors and what are the price expectations of the customers? All these marketing considerations lead to a managerial judgement as to what the market will bear in the face of prevailing competition, thereby determining the unit price to be charged to the customer. The volume corresponding to this unit price can then be estimated, so that the ensuing revenue now becomes 'given'.

As in the case of the cost-plus approach, the profit margin is again specified from the outset, to reflect what the financial community expects from the company in terms of financial performance, so that – in conjunction with the estimated volume – the unit profit can also be ascertained. With revenue and profit regarded as 'given', the total cost that can be tolerated is derived from the formula, which then tells management the level of unit cost that must not be exceeded. The resultant figures for unit cost and total cost become the objectives that operating managers have to achieve.

Three alternative managerial philosophies

So there you have it. Three formulations of the same basic simple relationship summarize three different managerial philosophies. The first, which sees profit as the final result of almost independent and almost self-contained corporate activities (namely production and sales), may be termed 'the opportunistic approach'. The management control process delineates the tasks that various departments in the organization need to perform and all those concerned are encouraged to do their best in their own prescribed areas of responsibility: the sales function is required to maximize the sales revenue, while the production function is required to keep a tight control on costs, the expectation being that if both functions perform well, the resultant profit would be satisfactory. The stochastic nature of the revenue and cost variables, however, causes excessive variability of the outcome, whereas most analysts prefer low risk and steady growth as good indicators of corporate stability.

The degree of uncertainty surrounding the profit level and profit margin can, of course, be greatly reduced by adopting 'the cost-plus approach', epitomized by the second formula. This management philosophy, which has long been the hallmark of some industries, is obviously of great benefit to the companies concerned, because it relieves them of bearing any risk by transferring it to their customers. Contract work for governments, for example in large civil engineering projects or in the field of defence, is typical of the supplier–customer relationship that has been prevalent for many years, with the customer picking up the tab, whatever the cost, and paying the supplier a guaranteed profit margin. In fact, such a philosophy – far from encouraging any competition and desire for efficiency – provides a clear incentive to the contractor to increase the cost of his operations, since the greater the cost of each contract, the greater his profit. The history of defence contracts in recent years is full of examples of gross inefficiencies and profligate financial management, and it is therefore not surprising that government financial auditors have become increasingly wary of cost-plus contracts.

The shortcomings of the opportunistic approach embedded in the first formula and the cost-plus mentality implied in the second have led to the third formulation, which may be called 'the market-oriented approach', where the starting point is the customer and the price that he is willing to pay. In a free market environment, it is the customer and the competition that drive the company to become more efficient and control its costs.

The third formula aims at eliminating the risk for the customer, and from his point of view the notion of having the final price as 'given' provides the most attractive formulation. This is not to say, though, that this formulation is also the 'best' solution for management for all products and all markets. For example, in the field of construction of large-scale one-off projects, particularly on an extended time scale, work on an agreed fixed-price basis (which is what this formula would entail) would place the risk of escalating costs entirely on the contractor, even when the escalation is totally outside his control.

It may, therefore, be argued that the third formulation is most applicable when a product is manufactured in volume, where alternative design specifications can be drawn up, depending on what price the market would bear, and where consequently the cost elements can be predicted with a reasonable degree of confidence. However, the element of risk for the manufacturer, when it comes to predicting the total cost and the unit cost, still remains, since the total cost and unit cost in volume production significantly depend on the volume of demand, particularly in industries with heavy capital expenditure and relatively high fixed costs.

Concluding remarks

Profit is understandably one of the key measures of financial performance, but the pursuit of profit has profound implications, which are further examined in the next chapter. The alternative presentations of the simple profit formula in this chapter illustrate how the same reality can be viewed from different angles and how perceptions of constraints can have far-reaching consequences for management philosophy and corporate strategy. There may very well be other simple managerial statements that we tend to take for granted, and if we stand them on their head, so to speak, we may well gain some fresh and challenging insights.

Alas, it is evident from watching managers in action that they are obsessed with constraints which circumscribe freedom of action and impede initiative, instead of realizing that (as indicated in the previous chapter) most constraints are self-inflicted, largely by the managerial hierarchy, in the form of budgets that must not be violated and targets that must be met. The imposition of constraints on lower echelons in the hierarchy is a natural managerial process, and we shall discuss it further as the philosophy of 'divide and rule' in Chapter 13. What we need to realize, though, is that managerial attention, particularly at the top level, is best focused on delineation of opportunities, rather than on constraints, and on examination of ways in which new opportunities can be created.

CHAPTER 7

The bottom-liners

Profit and economic growth

It wasn't such a long time ago when industrialists in the UK were distinctly uncomfortable, even apologetic, whenever the word 'profit' was mentioned. A vocal collection of sceptics in the wide area of business ethics combined into a chorus of disapproval, challenging the prevailing notions of the role of profit in society. Some of the protagonists were trade unionists, some were political activists for whom the capitalist industrial ethos was anathema, others were apprehensive about the growing power of international and multinational companies, and others still were concerned about the effect that a single-minded quest for economic growth would have on the environment and on the quality of life.

The backgrounds and aspirations of these groups were quite diverse, but they united in their criticism of the profit motive and saw it as a single manifestation of something that had gone badly wrong in Western societies. The sporadic rise of green parties in Western Europe, and the efforts devoted by politicians to social and environmental legislation, are further indications of the growing public concern.

To put it crudely, the critics of continuous economic growth regarded profit as representing some form of exploitation, supposedly carried out in the name of progress, but for the purpose of lining the pockets of shareholders and financiers: exploitation of the workforce, exploitation of customers, and exploitation of the environment. I remember the amazement with which my friends across the Atlantic greeted these sentiments and concluded that they were clear signs of decadence and impending economic decline. Growth coupled with profit had been accepted in North

America as an essential fuel for prosperity for so long that any voice of dissent was regarded at best as somewhat amusingly eccentric, if not downright treacherous to the fundamental tenets of Western civilization.

Needless to say, the climate of opinion has changed dramatically in recent years. First, doubts regarding uncontrolled growth and concern for the environment are now commonplace and voiced everywhere. Strong lobbies have sprung up even in the USA to question, control and constrain the profit aspirations of large corporations. At the same time, the climate in the UK and other Western countries – prompted by political and economic measures taken by successive governments in response to increasing pressures of global competition and its effect on prospects of employment and future prosperity – has become more attuned to the ideas of the market economy and is more sympathetic to goals involving economic success. Consequently, the stark contrast between attitudes across the Atlantic has been substantially eroded in recent years.

Furthermore, the mood in many countries in the Eastern bloc has also begun to move in the same direction. Western-type economic values are now propounded with increasing fervour, values such as efficiency, productivity and profit. Some of these trends have been discernible for some time, well before the recent changes in the Soviet Union, as visitors to Hungary and Yugoslavia even two decades ago would attest.

In China, too, attitudes have changed. A few years ago, I gave a lecture on corporate performance to an attentive audience in Beijing and was in the midst of explaining the intricacies of revenue and cost models as a prelude to a discussion of corporate performance criteria. I was trying desperately not to offend the sensibilities of my hosts and kept on referring to the concept of Surplus, which results from the difference between Revenue and Cost (as discussed in the previous chapter). Eventually, the exasperated translator turned to me and said: 'I think that what you mean is profit. We all know about profit', and proceeded to assure me that profit was no longer a dirty word in China.

So, everybody is at it. Everybody acknowledges that corporate performance matters, that a healthy business and industrial sector is essential in order to improve social wellbeing, so that all the parties involved – government, financial institutions, management and trade unions – need to create the necessary conditions for sustained progress, albeit within defined constraints to protect society and the rights of individuals. This broad goal is now widely shared by all concerned and is commonly found in many countries. The question that remains is that of interpretation and the means by which it should be achieved.

Common performance measures

One of the striking features of the current industrial philosophy in some countries (notably the USA and the UK) is the identification of certain financial measures as key indicators of corporate perform-ance, and these become objectives to be relentlessly pursued. Typical measures (although there are many others) include: profit, profit margins, return on investment, return on assets or equity, and earnings per share, which (for quoted companies) are reflected in their *P/E* (profit-to-earnings) ratio. The shortcomings of some of these criteria and the relationships between them are discussed further in the next two chapters. What is striking about all these measures is that they have one thing in common: They are related to a *short-term perspective*, largely based on annual or semi-annual company results, and these published reports are avidly read by stockbrokers, financial analysts, investors and lenders. Their reac-tions, in turn, profoundly affect the companies' future prospects, sometimes their independence and even their very survival.

Company directors are naturally conscious of these potential effects and hence they anxiously scour media reports and commen-taries in order to assess the mood and expectations of the financial markets. Inevitably, this affects their behaviour. As pointed out in the last chapter, the effect of these external pressures often causes annual accounts to be 'dressed up', so that the financial results appear in the best possible light. Anticipated income streams are brought forward for inclusion in the current financial year (and the converse also happens, when some income is set aside for inclusion in the next year, in order to avoid having to declare profit peaks and troughs), decisions to expand or to invest in new facilities are postponed or cancelled, training is seen as an unnecessary luxury –

all these actions are calculated to elicit the most favourable response from financial analysts, in order to achieve a high credit rating and a high share price.

The accounting gymnastics that sometimes take place prior to the release of the annual report are truly astounding, and although the manipulations may well be strictly legal, they tend to project an overoptimistic picture of the state of the enterprise. It is amazing (perhaps it is not amazing after all) how often a company subject to a hostile take-over suddenly manages to declare a remarkable leap in profit after a long series of indifferent annual results, clearly in the hope of winning the loyalty of shareholders and causing the take-over bid to fail. With a high rating in the City, or in Wall Street, the company becomes less vulnerable to would-be predators, it gets easier access to funds at advantageous terms, it can use its own paper for expansion and acquisitions, and its directors become more secure in their jobs.

No wonder they constantly ask themselves: 'What is the City (or Wall Street) looking for? What are the managerial actions that would impress the analysts most, and over what time horizon? What measures do we have to take to make it too expensive for outsiders to put a package together and mobilize the funds needed to bid for our company? In short, what are the criteria that will make us secure, and what actions do we need to take to meet these criteria?'

The bottom line

Alas, there seems little doubt that the answer invariably proffered is *concentration on the short term*, namely on the so-called 'bottom line'. The bottom line (which usually refers to profit, but may encompass some of the other performance criteria mentioned earlier), as shown in the most recent published accounts, is regarded by analysts as the best tangible evidence of what a company has achieved, and therefore a sensible guide (after taking account of general trends in the industry and the economy) of what it can achieve. The market has come to regard the bottom line as the most reliable measure of a company's current and future worth.

Although short-termism, as it has come to be called, has been attacked in the UK and the USA in recent years as the most pernicious attitude among industrialists and financiers in its negative effect on investment policies, there are strong dissenting voices. Marsh (1990), in a study sponsored by the Institutional Fund Managers Association in the UK, argues that he has found little evidence that connects decisions of professional investors with the perceived low level of investment in the UK and in the USA compared with that prevailing in Japan and Germany. He further argues that high-growth industries, such as pharmaceuticals and telecommunications manage to attract higher ratings among investors than those assigned to clearing banks and other conventional sectors of the economy. Lack of investment in industry is attributed by some commentators more to the low level of profitability of industry than the prevalence of short-termism.

I find these arguments quite unconvincing. Analysis of how investors and lending officers make decisions suggests that they are largely guided by such criteria as profit in the short term and the speed with which the initial investment or loan can be paid off, guided by techniques of discounted cash flow (which we discuss below).

A further assertion is that 'if short-termism is defined as the failure to undertake profitable long-term investments, then the perpetrators are not investment managers but industrial managers. The levers with power to maximise short-term profits, cutting investments, reducing operating costs or boosting revenues all lie in the control of the company executive' (Bell 1990).

This argument, too, is difficult to sustain. Industrial executives do not live in isolation wards. Their behaviour is bound to be conditioned by the attitudes of financial commentators, investors, shareholders, banks and other financial institutions. The economic environment in which industrialists operate is wedded to short-term results, and this is often expressed in incentive schemes that further encourage the beneficiaries to concentrate on the here and now.

The DCF protagonists

The consequence of this approach is that, since shareholders have the choice of pulling out and investing their money elsewhere, and since lenders are similarly wary of lending money to ailing companies (preferably they would like to lend to those who are so well-heeled that they do not need to borrow at all), corporate performance in the short term becomes a paramount objective for the CEO and his fellow directors. And so, industry on both sides of the Atlantic finds itself in the grip of the *philosophy of short-termism*. The bottom line, the here and now, is all that matters, and if actions in the short term have adverse consequences on the long term, so be it.

This is why DCF (discounted cash flow) has become so popular with managers considering proposals for investment appraisal. This method requires discounting all future cash flows, both costs and revenues, associated with a given proposed venture and consolidating them into a single NPV (net present value), to be compared with other investment alternatives. The DCF methodology can thus be used to rank the alternatives according to their NPVs, and the worthiness of each investment proposal can be judged by its individual NPV and by its associated measure, the IRR (internal rate of return), which is the discounting rate at which all discounted cash inflows are in balance with discounted investment outlays and costs. A specified minimum IRR, determined in relation to the cost of money and expectations of return on investment, provides a cut-off point, above which the IRR of a proposed investment is regarded as being worthwhile.

The dazzling attraction of this mechanistic approach has made DCF very popular not only in industrial circles, but has also led to its adoption as the basis for cost–benefit analysis as 'probably the form of decision analysis most commonly used by government and government agencies' (French 1986). French succinctly described the use of the methodology in the public sector as follows (1986: 370–1):

> The aim of cost–benefit analysis is to provide an objective financial evaluation of each alternative before it. To do this, it first identifies all the potential effects and their magnitudes. Then it costs each effect according to its value in the market place or in some surrogate market place. Finally it compares the net value of the benefits of the alternative with the net value of its detrimental effects. All the effects are reduced to financial values, however

intangible they might at first seem. It is the apparent objectivity with which this is done that is one of the method's strengths.... Unfortunately, the objectivity of cost–benefit analysis relies on certain assumptions that hide important value judgements. It assumes that it is possible to choose objectively the market place in which to value an effect. Yet, in fact, this choice is heavily laden with value judgements.

And he concludes that 'cost–benefit analysis does not make objective value judgements; it makes subjective ones obscure'. This often becomes quite evident when a cost–benefit exercise uses DCF methods in its attempts to quantify the costs and benefits involved.

Intangible costs and benefits

The sheer process of converting future tangible and intangible benefits into monetary values is fraught with arbitrary decisions. Take the example of a proposal to build a new motorway, the construction and maintenance costs of which are estimated by experts on the basis of past experience. These cost estimates prove at times to be notoriously unreliable, particularly in the case of large and complex projects, but this unreliability fades into insignificance when compared with assessments of the postulated benefits.

Leaving aside some benefits which are obviously difficult to quantify (such as the energy saving for those using the motorway resulting from better fuel consumption, the implications for vehicle depreciation and maintenance, as well as the effect on the environment), the main expected tangible benefit is the relief of congestion, measured by a reduction in travel time. But what value is to be put on the time saved? For those travelling on business the average cost per hour to their employers could presumably be ascertained and used as a surrogate measure, but is it appropriate to equate the value per hour saved with the cost per hour, or should the opportunity cost (which can only be guesstimated) be used for the purpose? And what is the value of time saved by the non-business traveller, for example on a shopping expedition or on vacation? Any value put on such time saving is sheer conjecture.

Furthermore, the total amount of time saved by travellers on the proposed new road is primarily a function of the amount of traffic that it will bear, and traffic projections are notoriously difficult to make. In the case of the M25 motorway surrounding London the peak traffic intensity predicted by the planners to occur 10 to 15 years after completion of the project in fact materialized almost immediately, so much so that the M25 has become the most infamous daily traffic jam in the country. So much for time saving and its postulated value computations at the planning stage.

Take another example, that of installing a new computer for the police force to assist in routine duties and in the detection and prevention of crime. The capital cost of the installation and the running costs are thought to be relatively easy to ascertain, but this cannot be said about the benefits. What is the monetary value of finding a missing person, who without the computer installation would not have been found? Of preventing the anxiety to house-holders caused by burglaries? Of reducing the incidence of assault or rape?

These ramifications have naturally cast doubt about the validity of applying cost–benefit analysis in the public sector. But even in the industrial sector, when all the financial positive and negative future cash flows are known and specified in advance (so that the issue of converting benefits into monetary values does not arise), serious questions have to be asked about what discounting factor should be used over a horizon of 10–30 years, as well as about the implications of the very discounting procedure.

Analysts familiar with DCF calculations know full well that cash flows in the immediate future affect the NPV to a far greater extent than flows expected in the more distant future. For this reason, large-scale projects with a considerable financial outlay, involving construction over many years before a stream of revenues can be realized, are becoming more and more difficult to justify to investors and financial institutions, particularly at times of high interest rates. It has been suggested that if DCF techniques had been extensively applied in earlier decades, there would have been little support for many mining ventures, where the expected life span for extraction often stretches over 30–50 years (in some cases even longer). Mercifully, DCF was not used at the time, or perhaps decisions to invest were made in spite of low net present values as they would have been then, so that we can continue to benefit today from decisions made in the past.

A similar example is that of companies in the building materials industry, engaged in the extraction of sand and gravel for civil engineering construction and road building, where the life span of quarries used for extraction can vary from 5–25 years, depending on the volume and quality of the deposits. In planning its extraction activities, a company needs to line up future quarry sites, which will come into operation when deposits in current quarries are exhausted. The acquisition of new sites depends on their availability (which is generally quite unpredictable) and on permission for extraction being granted by local planning authorities.

This means that sites may have to be acquired several years before they become productive, and during all this time the cost of acquisition (plus the interest on the loans taken for the purpose) and maintenance of the sites detract from their NPV. A company that decides, because of DCF considerations, to refrain from purchasing new sites when they become available, and waits instead until its current quarries are exhuasted, may find that it runs out of production capacity and that its future viability and even existence are then seriously jeopardized.

Another area where the DCF methodology can severely damage the future health of a company is that of skill training and management development (which were discussed briefly in the previous chapter). A management development activity, which can involve large expenditure, both in setting up the programme and in maintaining it, carries the risk that individuals would take advantage of their newly acquired skills to find jobs elsewhere, perhaps even with the competitors. It is not uncommon to find managers who use this argument for cutting down on their training budgets, particularly as it also helps them to improve their short-term financial performance.

The problem of using DCF is further compounded when future estimated costs are subject to a great deal of uncertainty. The production of a new aeroplane (such as Concorde) and the construction of large civil engineering projects (such as the Thames Barrier and the Channel Tunnel) are familiar examples of rapid cost escalations, which were unforeseen at the planning stage and which subsequently played havoc with the initial DCF projections.

The question that concerns many commentators is whether the current engulfing mood of short-termism will allow industry to invest for the future. That this mood has become so prevalent in the West can be seen from the curricula of most business schools, where DCF and cost–benefit analyses are often flogged to death and where students are taught to spot opportunities for making a fast buck. Not long ago one school has even proudly announced that it has had its whole curriculum revamped and that its prime aim is to teach students to become 'effective bottom line managers'. It is difficult to imagine a more cogent example of a total lack of appreciation of the future needs of industry, all this in response to the pressures of short-termism, instead of educating future managers to plan for long-term growth and prosperity.

Research and development

Needless to say, R&D (Research and Development) activities are *a priori* suspect to all bottom-liners: the amounts to be spent are large and uncertain, the probability of success is unknown and the prospects of exploitation are dubious. There is often a distinct risk that a new idea or a new design would fail altogether, either technically or commercially, and at the very least that it would take much longer to develop than originally anticipated. The combination of these three undesirable factors – heavy expenditure well before revenue begins to flow, volatility of the time span and the money required for results to materialize, and the risk of technical or commercial failure – is sufficient to kill many prospective projects stone dead.

For this reason, many companies prefer others to take the risk of investing in R&D and are content to be followers, and to copy the pioneers, once the new technology or product has proved itself. This policy of risk averseness is undoubtedly beneficial in its impact on the bottom-line in the short term, but in some cases the long-term effects – for example, in the pharmaceutical industry – may prove to be catastrophic, when the competitors succeed in cornering the market with brand-new products.

A chief executive of a company in the aerospace industry told me how every year he used to drag two dozen analysts from the City to show them his plant and product design centre, and particularly his R&D laboratories, of which he was immensely proud. He took pains to explain to the analysts the nature and significance of the various R&D projects, their novelty and potential impact on product design, all in the hope that the analysts would gain a better understanding of the activities of the company and a better appreciation of the need for a new range of products. Invariably, he said, the day after the visit he was hoping for favourable press comments and invariably he found that the shares of the company were marked down. It was clear that the analysts were positively put off by research and development in this industry. For them it was good money spent without any assurance of whether it would ever come back. In the short term they considered the expenditure detrimental to the bottom-line results.

It has to be said that short-termism is an affliction that is particularly prevalent in the West and in some of the emergent industrial countries in the Far East. Japanese industry seems to be working on much longer time horizons (and to a lesser extent this applies to Germany as well), and evidence from some Japanese companies suggests that strategic and corporate planning exercises over a period of ten or twenty years are by no means uncommon. There are many examples of Japanese companies being prepared to be very patient, and even lose a great deal of money for a long while, as part of their tenacious campaigns to penetrate potentially lucrative markets in the USA and Europe, where their presence now is almost taken for granted.

Even at Japanese low interest rates, many of these campaigns would not have passed the DCF test (if, indeed, it was ever applied), but looking at their dominant position now, few Japanese managers would have much cause for regret. It would seem that the attitudes and aspirations of the banks and financial institutions in Japan, with their heavy involvement as shareholders in industry, are much more oriented towards long-term strategic scenarios (arguably with overt or covert support from their government), so that companies are relieved from the bottom-line pressures that afflict their counterparts in the West. Perhaps there is a lesson there to be learnt about the need for short-term actions to be a part of a long-term strategy. As Shakespeare's Richard III said: 'Here will I lie tonight; but where tomorrow?' (Act V, Scene 3).

Conclusion

The eternal conflict between the short term and the long term reminds me of the well-known story about an old man who was planting a carob tree in his garden. A passer-by asked him why he took the trouble, since he would surely not be around when the tree was expected to mature and bear fruit. The old man pointed to another tree in the garden, with many branches heavy with the weight of fruit, and said: 'Can you see that tree? It was planted by my father for me to enjoy, and I am now planting this tree, so that my son can enjoy its fruit in years to come.'

References

Bell, J. 1990. Short-termism case against industry. *The Times*, 7 November.
French, S. 1986. *Decision Theory*. Chichester: Ellis Horwood.
Marsh, P. 1990. *Short-termism on Trial*. London: Institutional Fund Managers Association.

CHAPTER 8

A misleading performance measure

The need for multi-criteria

Managers, financial analysts and academics are all agreed that the performance of a business system cannot be judged by a single measure and that it requires a variety of criteria. In the literature this has found expression in a bewildering array of techniques under the general umbrella of 'multi-criteria decision making', or MCDM for short, the purpose of which is to reconcile the demands imposed by diverse managerial objectives.

As indicated in an earlier chapter, the simplest way of dealing with this problem is to construct a weighted sum of the stated objectives. This is achieved by following procedures that eventually result in explicit or implicit trade-offs between the criteria, so that the weighted sum then represents the overall performance measure that management should strive to improve. Where the weights are difficult or impossible to ascertain in quantitative terms, other techniques have been proposed, for example by asking decision makers to resort to ranking real or hypothetical outcomes, as a means of evaluating the relative merits of alternative courses of action.

The attraction of a single criterion

All this is not new, and the extensive literature is evidence of the tireless research that has been undertaken (and still goes on), attempting to throw further light on this difficult area. In practice, however, all the literature on MCDM appears to have made little impact on the way in which decisions are made and evaluated. In the real world managers seem decidedly uncomfortable when faced with the need to specify trade-offs, or even preferences, and they are understandably reluctant to have their preferences interpreted in ways which might commit them in the future.

Perhaps this is the reason for latching on to a single criterion for performance evaluation purposes. They generally do so in the belief that the importance of the chosen criterion is so overwhelming, that it completely dominates all other considerations, and that if this criterion is satisfied, all others would 'by and large' be reasonably satisified as well, or could be ignored. The advantages for managerial control purposes of adopting a simplistic approach that focuses the minds of all concerned on a single measure are self-evident, and for many senior executives these advantages far outweigh the seemingly dubious benefits of constructing a sophisticated message to the managerial hierarchy, involving multi-dimensional measures and entailing the inevitable implementation of elaborate monitoring and complex control mechanisms.

It must be said that many senior executives dispute this line of reasoning and are at pains to explain that they remain committed to the concept of multi-criteria in most business situations. They argue that when a particular criterion is chosen for scrutiny, it is not analysed to the exclusion of other considerations, but as a means of gaining a better understanding of the behaviour of the system under their control, so that the possible effects of alternative courses of future action can be properly comprehended. 'The fact that I keep searching for ways of achieving a higher level of performance of the organization with respect to one criterion', said one businessman, 'does not necessarily mean that it is my only objective, or the sole basis for making decisions. Obviously, I take other factors into account, and sometimes I make choices that do not maximize the outcome with respect to this criterion.'

Be that as it may, the fact remains that in many instances in industry, and in spite of protestations to the contrary, a single criterion often dominates. It is invariably cited, both for planning purposes and for inter-firm comparisons; it becomes so ingrained in the organizational culture, that even senior managers soon forget (or do not even know about) the caveats expressed during the discussions that preceded the adoption of the said criterion. And the longer it has been around, the more self-evident and immutable it becomes.

Return on equity (ROE)

This phenomenon was brought home to me the other day when I studied the operations of a merchant bank which is a constituent of a large banking group. When the question of performance measures came up, the senior executives singled out ROE (Return on Equity) as the criterion by which the overall performance was measured, both for the group as a whole and for all its subsidiaries, including our merchant bank.

ROE is simply the ratio of profit (for the sake of simplicity let us assume that it is pre-tax profit) to the value of the equity. Bearing in mind that this ratio is widely used in the banking sector in many countries, and that this criterion is cited both for monitoring changes in performance of a given institution over time and in performance comparisons between banking institutions, the choice of ROE in the case of our bank was not surprising.

When pressed as to why they thought that ROE was an appropriate criterion, the executives repeated the following stock argument. When an investor makes a decision where to invest, one of the main concerns (leaving aside considerations of risk, volatility and future expectations) is the return that he would get for his investment. This return is interpreted as the ROE, and if this ratio is poor, the investor would be tempted to put his money elsewhere.

Questions about ROE

Now, this argument raises many questions. First, strictly speaking, the measure of profit in the ROE ratio represents the profit to the enterprise, not to the investor; his return is the dividend, and the total amount of the declared dividend is usually lower than the corporate profit. It is true, of course, that any retained profit after payment of dividends to the shareholders increases the value of the assets of the enterprise, so that a share held by an investor should increase in value as well, and in theory the return to the investor for each share is the sum of the dividend and the retained profit per share (again, tax considerations are ignored for the sake of simplicity). In practice, however, the retained profit may not be reflected by an equivalent change in the share price, for a variety of reasons, so that ROE is not an accurate measure of the return to the investor.

The second question arises from the fact that the value of the equity is measured by the share price quoted on the stock exchange. This means that the ROE ratio has a numerator that changes infrequently (usually profits are declared every six months), whereas the denominator changes constantly, depending on the volatility of trading, on other factors that affect share prices in the industry, and on the state of the economy as a whole. As the denominator changes, so does the ROE ratio, so that the rise or fall in the ROE value may depend solely on the share price and not on the profit performance of the enterprise. We therefore have to face the paradox that while the ROE ratio is primarily intended by those who use it to measure the performance of the enterprise, most of the time it does nothing of the kind, since between profit declarations the fluctuations in the value of the ROE may be completely outside the control and influence of the management.

ROE for a subsidiary company

These considerations alone are sufficient to cast doubt about the appropriateness of this ratio as the sole, or even primary, measure of corporate performance. But in the case of a subsidiary company the problem is compounded by the need to ascertain its profit and equity value. Determining the profit of a subsidiary may be regarded as straightforward enough, since all subsidiaries are required to produce profit and loss accounts, but in practice much depends on what revenues and costs are attributed to any given entity. In many organizations, revenues may be the outcome of the combined efforts of several subsidiaries, as well as the active intervention of head office, so that determining what revenue is generated by any particular subsidiary may not be as obvious as it seems.

Similarly, the costs recorded in the profit and loss account follow the adopted accounting conventions for internal expenditure and overhead allocations, as reflected by internal transfer pricing practices (more on this vexed problem in Chapters 11 and 12). Thus, the distribution of revenues and costs (and hence profits) among the subsidiaries involves a wide range of arbitrary decisions, influenced by numerous internal and external considerations, so that the final figures attributed to a given subsidiary may be a gross distortion of the truth (whatever the 'truth' under these circumstances actually means).

So much for the credence that can be put on the officially declared profit of a subsidiary. Let us now turn to the value of its equity, which is needed for the denominator in the ROE ratio. In some organizations the value of the equity of part of the business is assumed to be proportional to the fixed assets allocated to that part, and these are determined by their book value. Since the total book value of the group is known (as recorded in the company books), and as the total equity value of the company can be determined by the prevailing share price, a pro-rata allocation of the equity value in proportion to the fixed assets can then be easily computed.

The problem with this procedure is that real assets are not necessarily directly related to fixed assets. Some parts of an organization make much greater demands on fixed assets than others, for example in the form of manufacturing plant and acccommodation, so that the resultant allocation of fixed assets bears little relationship to the true value of a subsidiary, namely the monetary value that could be realized if the subsidiary were to be disposed of. A profitable merchant bank, for example, has its main assets in the quality, skill and ingenuity of its personnel, not in the office machinery and furniture listed in the fixed assets book. To determine the equity value of the merchant bank in the manner described above is, therefore, both arbitrary and meaningless, so that any comparison of its ROE with other banks is devoid of any substance.

Further reservations

As if these doubts about the measurement methodology were not enough to call into question the whole basis of using ROE for the merchant bank, our scepticism was confirmed when it came to determining the equity value for the whole banking group. It transpired that the shares were not quoted on the stock exchange but that the group was wholly owned by an insurance company. It had bought the stock some years back and there was, therefore, no basis for determining the real value except by putting the group up for sale, or by asking hypothetical buyers how much they would be prepared to pay to acquire the group. Neither method was at all feasible, and it became clear that the total equity value for the whole group was no more than an arbitrary outcome of some obscure accounting conventions.

Thus, we started off in this case with a seemingly logical and highly structured procedure for determining the ROE ratio for a subsidiary: first, the equity for the whole group is ascertained, then it is allocated to the subsidiaries in proportion to the fixed assets; then the revenues and costs for each entity are determined from its profit and loss account, thereby providing its profit figure, and a simple final calculation then yields the ROE. However, a close examination of the measurement process involved in each of these steps causes the whole edifice to crumble. The resultant figure is evidently meaningless. It makes you wonder not only whether this elaborate exercise is worth the effort involved, but about the degree to which senior executives can be seriously misled and base their actions on spurious information.

Clearly, problems of veracity and interpretation of data do occur in the measurement process, whatever the chosen criteria, and in some cases the arbitrary nature of the accounting conventions lead to greater distortions than in others. But perhaps the lesson to be learnt is that a single criterion, however important, cannot be relied upon to provide an adequate picture of corporate performance. It also suggests that the more certain criteria are accepted as gospel truth, perhaps because of tradition and common practice, the more reason there is to scrutinize them and question their validity, the manner in which they are measured, and the use to which they are put.

CHAPTER 9

Prominent performance ratios

Criteria for corporate performance

In the previous chapter we considered the shortcomings inherent in using a single measure of corporate performance and highlighted the pitfalls that may be encountered in its adoption for the purpose of evaluation and managerial control. We now turn to the case where managers and commentators are moved to employ a higher level of analytical sophistication through the use of several performance criteria.

Of the many criteria that can be delineated to measure and evaluate corporate performance, most analysts and professional managers prefer the use of ratios. Absolute values of many variables, such as profit, volume, revenue and costs, as well as many other key figures, are obviously important and are commonly quoted in corporate plans and company accounts. But absolute values are not enough. Whether they are employed to make comparisons of performance of a given company for different time periods, or of different companies for the same time period, they provide only a partial picture. For example, when the level of profit of a company rises to £1.1m, compared with £1.0m in the previous year, the management may feel pleased by this evident progress, but if the performance in the previous year was rather poor, when compared with that recorded by competitors of similar size in the industry, or when compared with the resources used by the company, then the modest rise from £1.0m to £1.1m may not be sufficient cause for celebration.

This is why evaluation of corporate performance generally relies on ratios. The advantage of using a ratio is that it expresses the relationship between two variables, for example, between an

89

output and an input, or between various outputs (the product mix), or between various inputs (the resources mix). Tracking changes in the values of ratios over time, or comparing ratios for several plants in the same industry, provides managers with an analytical framework for constructing hypotheses about the causes for decline or improvement in corporate performance, so that lessons can then be learnt for future activities.

But which ratios should managers monitor and analyse? There is no unanimous answer among accountants and business analysts to this simple question. The literature abounds with a vast number of ratios to suit a variety of tastes and preferences, and this is evident from the different ratios selected for emphasis in different company accounts. Ask managers what they look for in making judgements about the performance of their companies, or that of their competitors, and you are astounded by the variety of answers that you get.

Return on capital employed

If pushed hard to choose only one single criterion, the expectation is that most managers and analysts will probably agree on ROCE (Return On Capital Employed) as the ultimate measure of corporate performance, in that it highlights the financial outcome (profit) against the total financial resources employed by the company. But, as pointed out in earlier chapters, most managers and analysts would also agree that any selected single measure gives an incomplete picture of the performance of an industrial enterprise.

For one thing, any ratio brings together only two entities from a wide array of inputs and outputs that characterize the whole range of activities of an enterprise. For another, the ROCE ratio is presumably constructed for the purpose of carrying out a comparative analysis, but in computing ROCE we often encounter measurement problems that may cast doubt about the validity of the comparisons made. The denominator of ROCE expresses the value of the total capital employed, an important component of which is the fixed assets of the company, but their value may well depend on the accounting conventions in use, and on whether book value has any relation to the value of the company assets in reality. Very often, book value is based on the purchase price of the assets and on outmoded and unrealistic depreciation procedures, which ignore the effect of inflation and changes in price movements (a common example of that relates to the value of property), so that when a revaluation exercise is undertaken, the book value of the fixed assets is often subjected to a significant adjustment, and this is then reflected in a drastic change in ROCE. Needless to say, such an adjustment may be totally unrelated to the way the company has conducted its activities, but is merely the outcome of a change in the measurement procedure.

This is why most league tables (compiled by various business magazines and financial analysts) avoid reliance on a single measure and typically record ten to twenty ratios to present performance statistics, although managers and commentators find such a large number of ratios too confusing and their attention tends to concentrate on a much smaller set of key ratios (sometimes on a single criterion, as in the example highlighted in the previous chapter).

It is important to bear in mind that performance ratios are not independent descriptors of an enterprise and that many are inter-linked; consequently, when one or two criteria, selected for special attention, show signs of improvement from one time period to another, this does not necessarily mean that other criteria have improved as well. In fact, the opposite may be the case. The following discussion centres on several examples to illustrate this point.

Three prominent ratios

After scanning the literature on corporate strategy, one is left with the impression that the following three ratios are perhaps the most popular with managers and commentators: (1) *ROCE*, (2) *the net profit margin* and (3) *the assets turn* (Eilon 1988). Many strategy consultants concerned with corporate performance evaluation also emphasize the significance of these ratios as the hallmarks of success, and clients are invariably urged to seek ways of improving all three.

What is not made sufficiently clear in the literature or in consultants' reports is that the three ratios do not always move in unison and that circumstances often arise when an improvement in one ratio can only be achieved at the expense of a deterioration in another. Let us start with the definitions of the three ratios, which for the purpose of this discussion, can be formulated as follows:

$$\text{ROCE} = \text{Net profit} / \text{Capital employed} \quad (1)$$

$$\text{Profit margin} = \text{Net profit} / \text{Revenue} \quad (2)$$

$$\text{Asset turn} = \text{Revenue} / \text{Capital employed} \quad (3)$$

The advantage of increasing each of these ratios seems self-evident. As stated earlier, the first ratio (namely, ROCE) is generally considered the ultimate measure of profitability and an increase in this ratio implies that the enterprise has managed to achieve a higher level of profit for a given input of total financial resources, or to achieve a given profit for a smaller resource input, or some combination of both. The second ratio, that of profit margin, is the proportion of the revenue that is retained after all the expenses (except for tax) have been accounted for. The third ratio is a measure of the trading activity of the company, showing the amount of sales that is achieved per unit of total capital employed.

Now, it is clear from these definitions that the three ratios are interconnected, as indicated in Figure 9.1, where each of the three entities shown on the left (profit, revenue and capital employed) affects the values of two of the three ratios shown on the right, so that the interdependence of the three performance ratios can be derived from the above definitions as follows (Eilon 1988):

$$\text{ROCE} = \text{Profit margin} \times \text{Asset turn}$$

or $\quad$ Ratio (1) = Ratio (2) × Ratio (3) $\quad\quad$ (4)

This relationship is shown graphically in Figure 9.2, where the coordinates represent ratios (2) and (3) respectively while ratio (1) is depicted by the iso-ROCE curves. Thus, the curve for ROCE = 30%, for example, is the locus of all points for that level of ROCE,

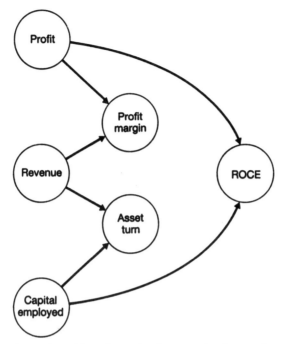

Figure 9.1   The relationship between the three ratios

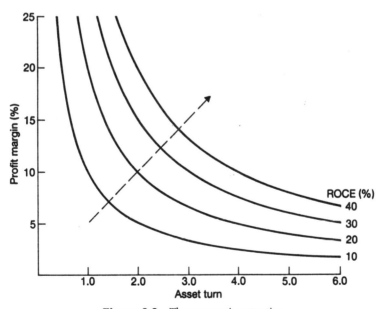

Figure 9.2   Three prominent ratios

and any point on the curve corresponds to a combination of profit margin and asset turn that yields a return on capital employed of 30%.

The arrow in Figure 9.2 signifies the direction in which strategy consultants urge their clients to move, since any change along this arrow achieves the objective that all three ratios increase in value. One way of reading equation (4) is to say that ROCE is the outcome of whatever values are achieved for ratios (2) and (3), so that if management succeeds in increasing the profit margin and the asset turn (as indicated by the arrow), then a higher ROCE would automatically be achieved.

Implications for managerial action

But what does this mean in terms of the three basic entities from which the three ratios are constructed, namely profit, revenue and capital employed? In what direction should these entities change, if we want to increase the values of the three ratios? A limited answer to this question is summarized in Table 9.1, which shows the effect of a change in each of the entities on its own. Thus, if profit increases (while revenue and capital employed remain unchanged), the effect would be an increase in profit margin and in ROCE (shown by the plus sign). Similarly, a decline in capital employed on its own has a beneficial effect both on the asset turn and on ROCE, whereas an increase in revenue on its own has a beneficial effect on the asset turn, but an adverse effect on the profit margin.

The qualitative results in this table merely give an indication of the effect of change in the value of one of the three variables listed

Table 9.1 The effect of profit, revenue and capital (Eilon 1988)
(+ denotes an increase while − denotes a decrease)

Ratio	Profit margin (2)	Asset turn (3)	ROCE (1)
Profit	+	+	+
Revenue	+	−	+
Capital employed	−	+	+

on the left-hand side of the table ('other things being equal'). In reality, though, other things are never equal and none of the three variables changes on its own.

For example, the table suggests that when capital employed declines then asset turn and ROCE are expected to rise. But this is merely a sufficient, not a necessary, condition. In fact, when a company expands its operations in order to achieve higher sales, it may well have to increase the asset base in order to sustain the envisaged expansion. What the table tells us, though, is that an increase in the asset base, and hence in the capital employed, can adversely affect the ROCE ratio, unless the increase in the capital employed is accompanied by an even larger increase in profit, so that the final outcome for the three ratios does not depend on the *absolute changes* in the three listed variables, but on their *relative changes*. The plus and minus signs shown in the table do not, therefore, reveal the whole story in terms of the direction in which management should attempt to move.

Nevertheless, the table contains one interesting result, namely the effect of an increase in revenue, which appears, at the same time, to be both beneficial and detrimental for the asset turn and profit margin respectively. And herein lies the potential conflict that can emerge between the three ratios, demonstrating that it may be possible for one to improve at the expense of another.

Alternative scenarios and the concept of dominance

To illustrate this point, consider a company which has a profit of 10, a revenue of 100 and capital employed of 40, so that the three ratios are:

ROCE, i.e. ratio (1)   = 0.25, or 25%

Profit margin, i.e. ratio (2) = 0.10, or 10%

Asset turn, i.e. ratio (3)   = 2.5

This is shown as case A in Table 9.2. Now suppose that the company can continue to operate at the current level A or follow one of

Table 9.2 Five scenarios (Eilon 1988)

Case	Profit	Revenue	Capital employed	The three ratios (2) (%)	(3)	(1) (%)
A	10	100	40	10.0	2.5	25.0
B	13.5	108	36	12.5	3.0	37.5
C	14.6	112.3	74.9	13.0	1.5	19.5
D	6.0	120	30	5.0	4.0	20.0
E	13.7	160	45.7	8.6	3.5	30.0

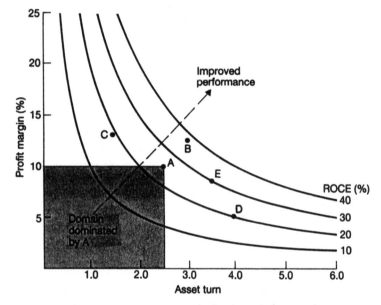

Figure 9.3 Five cases – which is best? (Eilon 1988)

several strategies, depicted by scenarios B, C, D and E. The various alternatives and their respective outcomes are shown in Table 9.2 and Figure 9.3. Which strategy should be adopted? (Note that the five listed cases may either correspond to different modes of operation of the same plant, or describe the performance of five different plants, in which case the question would be: which plant is considered best in terms of the three performance criteria?)

First, compare the current performance A with the scenario B. Clearly, B is better with respect to all three ratios. In fact, B may be said to dominate A, which in turn dominates any point in the shaded area below and to the left of A in Figure 9.3. The concept of dominance is generally very useful for ranking purposes, since it does not require us to specify any trade-offs between the three ratios, and whether all three ratios are regarded as equally desirable or not makes no difference to the conclusion that operating at point B is preferable to that at point A.

Consider, however, the other three cases in Table 9.2. In case C the profit level, the revenue and the capital employed are all higher than their respective values in cases A and B. The resultant profit margin of 13.0% for C is higher than for A; in fact, it is the highest of all the five scenarios shown in the table, but the values of the two other ratios are the lowest. In contrast, case D has the lowest profit in the table, as well as the lowest level of capital employed, resulting in the best asset turn, but the worst profit margin and almost the worst ROCE. Case E has the distinction of recording the highest level of revenue, but it does not come best in any of the three ratios.

The five cases are shown in Figure 9.3, from which it transpires that the only clear dominance relationship is between scenarios A and B, but not between any of the others. Thus, from the information available in Table 9.2, it is only possible to conclude that scenario B is better than the current operation A, but no other overall ranking clearly emerges, unless trade-offs between the three ratios are explicitly specified.

This conclusion is perhaps better demonstrated by focusing attention on the *relative changes in performance*, namely by the degree to which each performance measure changes in comparison with its original value (Eilon 1984). The curve shown in Figure 9.4 depicts the condition for ROCE to remain unchanged, so that the area above the curve corresponds to ROCE increasing in value, while the area under the curve corresponds to a decline in ROCE. The vertical ordinate measures the relative change in the profit margin; for example, if the original profit margin stands at 20% then a 10% increase brings the profit margin up to 22%. Any point above the origin corresponds to an increase in the profit margin and any point below the origin corresponds to a decline. Similarly, the abscissa measures the relative change in the asset turn, so that a point to the right of the origin signifies an increase in this ratio, and any point to the left accords with a decline.

The two coordinates in conjunction with the curve in Figure 9.4

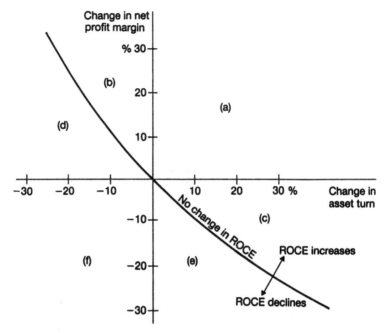

Figure 9.4 Effect of changes in net profit margin and asset turn on ROCE

create six domains, which exhibit the following interesting characteristics with respect to the three performance ratios:

(a) in this domain all three ratios increase in value and their
     movement corresponds to the arrow in Figure 9.2;
(b) here the profit margin increases while the asset turn declines,
     and the outcome is that ROCE increases;
(c) this domain is the mirror image of (b) and here the net profit
     margin declines while the asset turn rises, again resulting in an
     increase in ROCE;
(d) this domain is similar to (b), except that here ROCE declines;
(e) this domain is similar to (c), but ROCE declines;
(f) in this domain all three ratios decline.

    Thus, the domain (a) corresponds to the sufficient condition that
if both net profit margin and asset turn rise, then ROCE will also
rise, while domains (b) and (c) cover other circumstances when
ROCE rises. Similarly, domain (f) expresses the sufficient condition

that if both net margin and asset turn decline, then ROCE must also decline, while the remaining domains (d) and (e) relate to other circumstances when ROCE declines.

Furthermore, the diagram suggests that if either ratio (1) or (2) falls by a certain amount (in percentage terms), then the other must rise by a greater amount to compensate for this fall, if ROCE is to remain unchanged. For example, if the asset turn falls by 20%, the profit margin would have to rise by 25% for ROCE to remain at its original level. Note that this result is quite independent of the original values of the three ratios (a more detailed discussion of such outcomes can be found in Eilon (1984)).

Other notable performance measures

The examples shown above relate to the three prominent strategic ratios defined earlier, but what has been demonstrated for these ratios can be extended to others, and it is not difficult to show that many of the criteria by which business performance is judged are not always compatible with each other, and sometimes are even in direct conflict. For our second example, we consider the relationships between two commonly used measures of profit margin. First, we need to take note of the following definitions:

> *Profit, or net profit*, is derived (see Chapter 4) as the difference between the sales revenue and the total cost (except for tax).
>
> *Operating profit, or gross profit*, takes account only of the operating costs (and excludes the fixed costs of the operations), that is, it equals the net profit plus the fixed costs.
>
> *Net profit margin* is the ratio of net profit to revenue (in the absence of any indication to the contrary, the term 'profit margin', as used earlier in this chapter, is interpreted to mean 'net profit margin').
>
> *Gross profit margin* is the ratio of the operating profit to revenue.

Both profit margin ratios are widely used in industry and commerce. The net margin is an acknowledged measure that reflects overall performance, whereas the gross margin is popular in certain industries, for example in retail and distribution, for pricing and measuring the profitability of individual products.

Consider now the following three general statements, commonly found in industry:

(a) Net and gross profit margin always go together, so that if the latter rises, the former is bound to rise as well.
(b) An increase in profit can only be achieved through an increase in revenue.
(c) An increase in revenue, provided it is also accompanied by an increase in profit, must result in an improvement in both net and gross profit margins.

All three statements, and many others of the same ilk, are fallacious, as will be demonstrated below.

Let us consider a general example (Eilon 1984), in which the net and gross profit margins in the basic scenario are 20% and 40% respectively, and assume that the fixed cost remains unchanged (i.e. it remains the same for the various scenarios or alternatives to be evaluated). A change in unit price affects the revenue and a change in volume affects both the level of revenue and total cost. These changes affect the profit level and in turn the performance ratios are affected, as shown in the diagram of network relationships in Figure 9.5.

It can be shown that four indifference curves can be drawn for this general case to demonstrate the behaviour of four major criteria, namely *revenue, profit, net profit margin and gross profit margin*, and these four curves are shown in Figure 9.6:

- The first is the locus of all points for no change in the gross profit margin (this curve coincides with the abscissa): an increase in unit price (corresponding to any point above the horizontal line) causes the gross profit margin to increase, while a reduction in price causes it to decline).
- The second curve corresponds to no change in the net profit margin (again, the areas above and below the curve signify an increase and decrease in the net margin respectively).
- The third curve corresponds to no change in profit.
- The fourth curve corresponds to no change in revenue.

100

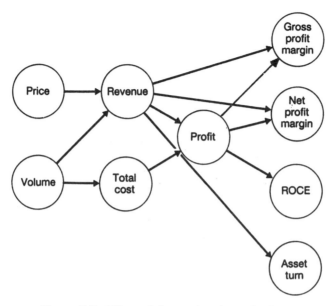

Figure 9.5 Effects of changes in price and volume

Ten scenarios, in addition to the base case, are listed in Table 9.3 to illustrate how these four performance measures can diverge. The second and third columns in the table show the changes (in %) in unit price and volume from the base case, and the last four columns show the corresponding results (the figures in these columns have been rounded off) for revenue, profit, and the two profit margins. In five cases the volume increases by 15% compared with the base case, while in five cases the volume falls by 15%.

From Figure 9.6 and the scenarios in Table 9.3 we may draw the following conclusions:

1   If both volume and unit price increase, namely we are concerned with the first quadrant of Figure 9.6, then all the four measures improve (see example A in Figure 9.6 and Table 9.3). Similarly, if both volume and unit price decline, all the four measures deteriorate (as illustrated by the example K).

2   In the quadrant where volume declines but unit price increases, an improvement in revenue (i.e. above the line corresponding to no change in revenue) certainly results in an increase in the other three measures (example F); in fact, it is even possible for

101

Table 9.3 Ten examples of the effect of changes
(base scenario: net margin = 20%, gross margin = 40%)

Scenario	Price increase (%)	Volume increase (%)	Revenue	Profit	Profit margins (%) net	gross
Base	0	0	100	20	20	40
A	5	15	121	32	26	43
B	−2.5	15	112	23	21	38
C	−4.5	15	110	21	19	37
D	−8	15	106	17	16	35
E	−15	15	98	9	9	29
F	20	−15	102	31	30	50
G	10	−15	94	23	24	46
H	5.5	−15	90	19	21	43
J	2	−15	87	16	18	41
K	−10	−15	77	6	7	33

revenue to decline and yet for the other criteria to improve (example G), thereby contradicting statement (b) above; of particular interest is example J, where the gross margin increases in spite of the fact that revenue, profit and the net profit margin all decline.

3 In the quadrant where volume increases but unit price declines, the gross profit margin also declines. A fall in revenue in this quadrant corresponds to a decline in all the other three measures as well (see example E), but an increase in revenue is no guarantee of an improvement in the others (demonstrated by example D, for which profit and the two profit margins decline), clearly in contradiction to statement (c) above, unless the revenue increase is quite substantial (as demonstrated by examples B and C). Also, just above the line corresponding to no change in profit, we have the interesting outcome that both revenue and profit increase, but both profit margins decline (see example C).

4 Between the lines corresponding to no change the net margin and gross margin respectively there is a domain where one profit margin increases and the other declines, thereby contradicting statement (a) above (see examples B and J in Figure 9.6 and Table 9.3).

5 Along the abscissa there is no change in unit price, and as we can see from Figure 9.6 there is no change in the gross profit

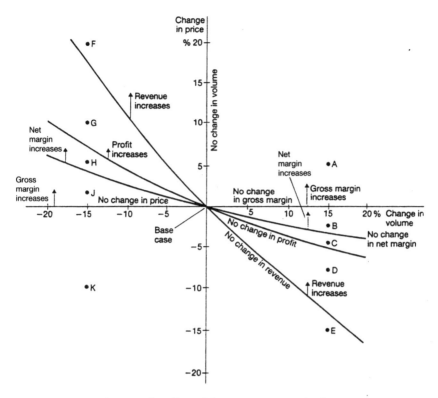

Figure 9.6 Effect of changes in price and volume

BASE CASE: NET PROFIT MARGIN = 20%
GROSS PROFIT MARGIN = 40%

margin either, irrespective of the change in volume. If the volume increases (i.e. if we move from the base case to the right in Figure 9.6), the net margin, revenue and profit all increase, and if the volume decreases (i.e. we move to the left), they all decline.

Conclusion

The examples in Tables 9.2 and 9.3 clearly demonstrate that prominent strategic ratios do not change in unison, and at times they even diverge. When they are not compatible with each other, an improvement in one can only be achieved at the expense of others. Under such circumstances, ranking multi-criteria scenarios (or the performance of several plants) is not possible without a clear indication of the relative desirability of the criteria in question, and this entails explicit or implicit statements about trade-offs.

The examples given here suggest that exhortations to managers to 'improve on all fronts' are too simplistic and that it is not always possible to translate them into clear managerial actions, even when the complex cause-and-effect relationships between the multitude of variables in a business system are fully understood, which in the majority of cases they are not.

The lesson to be learnt from all this is that corporate performance can rarely be reduced to a clear-cut black-and-white descriptor; more often than not, it comes in all shades of grey.

References

Eilon, S. 1984. *The Art of Reckoning – Analysis of Performance Criteria*. London: Academic Press.
Eilon, S. 1988. Three prominent performance ratios. *Omega* 16: 503–8.

CHAPTER 10

Use and misuse of productivity ratios

The importance of productivity

In the last few chapters we considered various financial ratios for evaluating corporate performance. In this chapter we turn to another set of important performance ratios, namely those associated with productivity. There is no denying that productivity is widely acclaimed as the prime factor that determines the level of prosperity and standard of living in most countries of the world, and consequently a great deal of managerial effort is expended on measuring and analysing productivity in industry.

Leaving aside a few countries richly endowed with natural resources, which can generate ample income to sustain even an indolent population in comfort, the economy of most countries and the wellbeing of their industries depend on how well they can use all their resources – manpower, materials, plants and money – to produce goods and services at an acceptable price and meet demand at home and abroad. The better the utilization of resources and the greater the output that can be generated from a given input (provided there is a demand for the output in question), the greater the wellbeing of the enterprise: it can cover its costs, it can improve the remuneration and working conditions of its employees, it can reward its investors, and it can modernize and expand.

Productivity is a term that encapsulates the quality of the conversion process from a series of resource inputs to a series of outputs, and – subject to satisfactory measurement criteria – it is taken for granted that an improvement in productivity is beneficial and must be relentlessly pursued.

The importance of the subject is exmplified by its continuous exposure in the economic and financial press, by inter-firm and international comparisons, by arguments between employers and trade unions, and by pious exhortations from politicians to us all to work harder and more intelligently to improve productivity. The professional literature in this area has also responded rapidly in recent years, though it has to be admitted that thorough and crucial exposés are not as plentiful as would befit such an important subject.

Some definitions

First, consider definitions. As Gold points out (Gold 1973; Eilon *et al.* 1976), productivity is commonly interpreted as output in terms of physical volume per employee or per man-hour, in other words it is equated with productivity of labour. Other inputs, such as materials and capital, are often ignored, and it is generally assumed that if productivity of labour increases, then other measures of performance will automatically benefit as a result.

Paul Mali recognizes this issue in his book entitled *Improving Total Productivity* (with the long-winded subtitle, 'MBO strategies for business, Government, and not-for-profit organizations'): 'Productivity requires resources such as plant capacity, personnel, costs, raw materials, facilities, capital, technology, budgets, supplies and information' and he proposes the following definition: 'Productivity is the measure of how well resources are brought together in organizations and utilized for accomplishing a set of results. Productivity is reaching the highest level of performance with the least expenditure of resources' (Mali 1978: 6–7). As for measurement, he proposes a productivity index in the form of a ratio (p. 21):

$$\text{productivity index} = \frac{\text{output}}{\text{input}}$$

$$= \frac{\text{performance achievement}}{\text{resources consumed}} = \frac{\text{effectiveness}}{\text{efficiency}}$$

and elsewhere (p. 212):

$$\text{productivity index} = \frac{\text{output}}{\text{input}}$$

$$= \frac{\text{performance achievement}}{\text{resources allocated}} = \frac{\text{actual performance}}{\text{expected performance}}$$

As a piece of algebraic formulation these definitions do not strictly hold, since 'resources consumed' may not be equal to 'resources allocated', nor is it valid to equate 'resources allocated' with 'expected performance'. We know, of course, what the author is driving at, but the lack of rigour in some of his definitions may adversely affect the whole process of measurement and evaluation. He rightly states that *productivity is a combination of effectiveness and efficiency* and proceeds to distinguish between the two (effectiveness is the degree to which end results are achieved and is output-oriented). But a definition that asserts that productivity is the ratio of effectiveness to efficiency (as stated above) is baffling, to say the least, since it implies that for a given level of effectiveness, productivity increases when efficiency declines, and this cannot possibly be what the definition intends to convey.

Alternative measures of productivity

In order to understand the basis for proposing alternative methods of measuring productivity, consider first the definition

$$\text{productivity of factor input X} = \frac{\text{output}}{\text{factor input X}}$$

which highlights the fact that many productivity ratios can be constructed, each relating to a particular disaggregated input, or to a combination of inputs. As for metric, the output may be measured either in physical terms (such as tons, kilowatts, or other appropriate units of physical output) or in financial terms (revenue, profit, or added value). Similarly, the input may be measured in physical

Table 10.1   Inputs and outputs

| | | OUTPUT | |
		Actual	Maximum
INPUT	Actual	1	2
	Minimum	3	

or cost terms (tons of material input, man-hours, cost of materials, cost of labour, value of fixed assets, etc.).

Secondly, it is necessary to determine what input and output should be considered, actual or optimal. The simple matrix in Table 10.1 shows the possible combinations that guide the selection of criteria. In cell 1 we consider the *actual output relating to an actual input*. Such a ratio on its own tells the analyst little about performance, since he (or she) is unable to state whether the ratio is good or bad. He therefore needs to compare it with a standard in order to make a judgement. This standard may be provided by:

- a ratio relating to a previous time period;
- a ratio relating to a similar activity carried out at the same time elsewhere (in the enterprise or outside), or to the industry as a whole (this is the essence of inter-firm comparisons);
- a ratio of the maximum output that can be obtained for a given level of input (cell 2 in the matrix);
- a ratio of the minimum input needed to produce the actual level of output (cell 3 in the matrix).

Thus, an evaluation of performance may be based on a comparison of ratio 1 with itself (for other time periods or for other operations), or with ratio 2, or with ratio 3.

This explicit formulation helps us to understand the many ramifications of the measurement process and it is, unfortunately, missing from Mali's book, though he does implicitly recognize these ratios in the diverse list that may be considered in several circumstances. As for the optimum output or input in cells 2 and 3, Mali strongly advocates the use of MBO (management by objectives) which – despite the shortcomings of its subjective nature – is still widely used in corporate planning and evaluation. What it boils down to is a comparison of *actual output with optimal output* (often referred to as the *capacity* of a plant with given resource inputs) or *optimal input with actual input*, as is clear from the following:

$$\frac{\text{Index 1}}{\text{Index 2}} = \frac{(\text{actual output}) / (\text{actual input})}{(\text{maximum output}) / (\text{actual output})}$$

$$= \frac{\text{actual output}}{\text{maximum output}}$$

$$= \frac{\text{actual output}}{\text{capacity}} = \text{capacity utilization}$$

$$\frac{\text{Index 1}}{\text{Index 3}} = \frac{(\text{actual output}) / (\text{actual input})}{(\text{actual output}) / (\text{minimum input})} = \frac{\text{minimum input}}{\text{actual input}}$$

The interesting facet of this approach is that although the definition of productivity starts with a ratio of output to input, a comparison of index I with index 2 involves a ratio of output to output and that of index 1 with index 3 a ratio of input to input. Furthermore, for any particular input, it is possible for the two comparisons to yield different results, even when MBO is used to specify both optimal inputs and outputs. A recognition of such conclusions by writers on productivity, illustrated by practical case studies, would be appropriate and helpful to practitioners grappling with planning and implementation of productivity programmes.

The importance of measurement leads Mali to identify five categories of ratios: overall indices, objective ratios, cost ratios, work standards and time-standard ratios. With 24 items in each category, his list covers 120 ratios, although the reader is warned that these are merely examples and that 'an endless variety is possible'. It is the case, however, that when faced with such a perplexing variety, the analyst would welcome some guidance. Surely, not all ratios are of equal importance. Some are likely to be more significant than others in their potential effect on certain global measures of performance, such as profit, return of investment, or total unit cost.

The elucidating structure proposed by Gold (1973) to show how productivity ratios are linked to these overall measures is sadly lacking in other texts on productivity analysis. Mali's treatise, for example, does not contain an explicit discussion of the intricate network of relationships between productivity measures and the fact that one can be improved at the expense of another. As Gold points out, increased productivity of one factor input (such as labour productivity) does not automatically result in decreased unit cost and may not in itself be desirable. It is only through a systematic examination of the relevant network of relationships that the consequences of changes in operating methods and factor prices can be properly assessed.

An example

It is worth examining a simple example, which illustrates many cases encountered in industry. This is presented in Table 10.2. An operation described under scenario A involves 100 employees producing a physical volume of 500 units, so that labour productivity stands at 5.00 per man. The total costs, consisting of cost of materials, labour costs and other expenses (overheads, depreciation, interest charges, etc.), amount to 600, so that the unit cost is 1.20. The selling unit price stands at 1.32, yielding a total revenue of 660. When the total costs are deducted from this revenue, the resultant profit is 60.

Now, under scenario B it is envisaged that volume would rise by 20% to 600 units, incurring an increase in manpower of only 8% (from 100 to 108), corresponding to labour productivity of

Table 10.2 An example of an increase in labour productivity

Scenario	A	B	Change (%)
Cost of materials	200	240	20.0
Labour costs	100	120	20.0
Other costs (overheads, depreciation, etc.)	300	400	33.3
Total cost	600	760	12.7
Volume (physical units)	500	600	20.0
No. of employees	100	108	8.0
Labour productivity (units/man)	5.00	5.56	11.1
Unit cost	1.20	1.27	5.6
Unit price	1.32	1.32	0
Revenue	660	792	20.0
Profit	60	32	−46.7

600/108=5.56 units per man, namely an increase of 11.1%. To achieve this increase in labour productivity, it is necessary to spend money on the plant, which would increase the overheads and other costs from 300 to 400. It is reasonable to expect the cost of materials to increase proportionately with the increase in volume, namely by 20%, from 200 to 240. If the employees are to be fully compensated for the increase in productivity, the labour costs would increase by 8% (to account for the increase in the number of employees) and by 11.1% (the increase in labour productivity), resulting in labour costs increasing from 100 in scenario A to 120 in scenario B.

Thus, the total cost in scenario B amounts to 760, so that the unit cost rises from 1.20 to 1.27, in spite of the increase in labour productivity. If the unit price remains unchanged, the result in scenario B is that revenue rises by 20% (in line with the increase in volume) to 792, but profit slumps to 32, almost to a half of its level under scenario A.

This example demonstrates that an increase in labour productivity on its own is not sufficient to improve corporate profitability. In this case, the rise in productivity is far too low to compensate for the significant increase in what is called in the table 'other costs', resulting in an increase in total unit cost, a decline in competitiveness and a decline in profit.

Some doubtful measures

That measures in isolation can be too parochial, even whimsical, and hence of rather questionable relevance, is evident from many cases encountered in industrial and administrative organizations, or even in the literature. To illustrate this point consider the following examples of ratios advocated in the literature (see Mali 1978: 88–9):

(a) Inventory/(advertising costs) is one of the suggested cost ratios, though it is none too clear what relationship there might be between the numerator and the denominator. The ratio can presumably be increased by increasing inventory levels and reducing advertising expenditure, but why should this be interpreted as an improvement in performance?

(b) (Recruits selected)/costs is a proposed measure in the

governmental sector, but recruiting cost per employee (which is the inverse of the above ratio) is usually minute compared with the subsequent costs of training and employment, so that it may in fact be beneficial to increase recruitment costs to improve the quality of intake, rather than embark on a cost-cutting exercise in order to improve this so-called productivity of personnel recruitment.

(c) (Students graduating)/(annual costs) is suggested as a suitable measure in the field of education, though again no reference is made to the quality of the output, which is obviously of prime importance, even if it is difficult to measure objectively. Clearly, it is possible to reduce the cost per student (the cost per graduating student is the inverse of the above ratio) by providing poor teaching and inferior facilities, and such moves in the name of efficiency are evident in some countries, though this can hardly be regarded as a desirable outcome.

(d) Graduates/curricula is a similar ratio in the field of education, to indicate the degree of success of a training or teaching programme. This ratio has been proposed as a 'work stan-dard', though its useful application in evaluating programmes is somewhat obscure.

(e) (Research reports)/(allocated budget) is a ratio cited as suit-able in the field of 'health and human services'. The naive notion that the number of research reports can in any way be a sensible measure of output is perhaps symptomatic of the degree of crudity with which some ratios can be constructed. A change in the value of such a ratio can hardly be indicative of a change in the utility, efficiency, or even the level of activity of a research group.

(f) Admission cost per patient per week in a hospital is quoted in a case study where additional office machinery helped to reduce staff and thereby total admission costs (Mali 1978: 57–8). However, a great deal depends on what is meant by 'admissions'. It is possible, of course, to reduce processing at the admission stage by deferring some of the work, which is usually carried out at the admission stage, to be completed elsewhere in the hospital at a later period. The result would be that the 'cost per admission' is reduced, but the total workload remains unchanged.

Some ratios are more sensible than others

There are other examples, but these suffice to support two arguments alluded to earlier: first, although in theory an infinite number of ratios is possible, in practice only 'sensible' control ratios ('sensible' in a managerial context) need to be considered; second, as illustrated in the various scenarios for corporate performance ratios in the previous chapter, it is usually not difficult to conceive of ways for improving a particular ratio at the expense of one or several others and it is therefore not immediately obvious that the overall outcome would be desirable.

All this tends to overshadow some of the positive aspects of what the literature on productivity can offer. Mali, for example, is particularly good on checklists, which can come in handy for practitioners as they become immersed in intricate and time-consuming investigations. His proposal that productivity audits should be conducted from time to time is a useful reminder that when executives are embroiled in the day-to-day running of their operations, they are generally incapable of standing back and evaluating performance in a wider context. He rightly insists that productivity measures need not be confined to the manufacturing environment, but can often be designed for a variety of service activities.

What is often missing, though, is a proper analytical framework, an attempt to bring together the various control tools through a network of relationships to provide a penetrating insight into the way that an enterprise functions (for example, in the way proposed by Gold (1973)), so that the causes of changes in past performance can be understood as a proper basis for postulating on the possible consequences of alternative managerial actions.

References

Eilon, S., Gold, B. and Soesan, J. 1976. *Applied Productivity Analysis for Industry*. Oxford: Pergamon Press.
Gold, B. 1973. Technology, productivity and economic analysis. *Omega* 1 (1): 5–24.
Mali, P. 1978. *Improving Total Productivity*. New York: Wiley.

CHAPTER 11

A cake can be cut in many ways

Criteria and models depend on data

The discussion in the previous chapters highlighted the need for reliable financial data as an essential ingredient for evaluation of performance and for decision making. As management control and executive action become increasingly dependent on feedback and on the quality of information relating to past performance, the importance of clear and consistent definitions of all the entities employed in monitoring performance criteria cannot be under-estimated. Inevitably, the measurement and monitoring process follows certain prescribed procedures, but as alternative methods may well affect the results, they need to be closely scrutinized, so that their relevance and impact can be better understood. In this chapter we look at one particular problem that has a bearing on the computation and meaning of financial data within the organization.

We saw in earlier chapters that many questions can be raised regarding the appropriate criteria with which the performance of an enterprise should be assessed. Here we are not concerned with the selection of overall criteria, but with the financial data used to compute these criteria, namely with the nuts and bolts that constitute the financial data bank.

Usually, analysts do not expect to get involved with the question of the appropriateness of stated objectives, regardless of whether they pertain to particular parts of an organization or to the organization as a whole. Objectives are generally regarded as the prerogative of senior management. In a sense, the relationship between manager and analyst is akin to that of a client and a professional adviser: The client tells the adviser what he (or she) wants to achieve, and the adviser proceeds to explore various

114

courses of action to that end. From time to time, the adviser is bold enough to question short-term objectives and whether they are compatible with long-term goals, in which case amendments to the stated objectives may be considered. But generally, it is accepted that the ultimate responsibility for deciding on objectives lies with management, and the analyst is expected to work within that framework. Objectives are thus taken as 'given'.

Another 'given' pertains to financial data, and most analysts take such data for granted. They focus their attention on the construction of analytical models, they examine the possible outcomes of feasible courses of action, they postulate on the consequences of certain scenarios; eventually, the analysis culminates with a set of conclusions and recommendations for management to consider.

Throughout this exercise, the implicit assumption is that the necessary financial data would be available to feed into the models and, apart from sensitivity analyses to determine the effect of some minor deviations from the assumed data on the computed results, the validity of the data is rarely challenged. What analysts and managers often fail to appreciate is the degree to which data are the product of adopted accounting conventions, so that different methods of treating various cost elements may well result in totally different interpretations, and hence lead to different conclusions. To illustrate this point, let us examine in this chapter the impact of using alternative conventions for allocating overheads.

Cost analysis for multi-products

Consider the following example. A company produces three products, and the basic financial data are summarized in Table 11.1.

Table 11.1 Basic cost and revenue data

Product	Fixed cost	Variable cost	Total cost	Revenue	Profit
1		80		400	
2		120		500	
3		200		700	
Total	1000	400	1400	1600	200

115

The direct cost associated with each product (usually referred to as 'variable cost') is known and shown in the table, the total variable cost being 400, but the fixed-cost overhead of 1000 is only recorded for the plant as a whole. The table also records the revenue obtained for each of the products, the total revenue amounting to 1600.

The information given in this table suggests that while the cost and profit for the total product mix are known, there is no breakdown of the cost and profit for the individual products. Similarly, the overall profit margin (defined as the ratio of profit to revenue) can be readily found (in this example the total profit is 200 and the total revenue 1600, so that the overall profit margin is 12.5%), but in order to ascertain the individual profit margins, it is necessary first to allocate the fixed cost to the three products, in order to calculate the cost and profit for each.

The accounting convention in this plant is to allocate the fixed cost to products in proportion to their variable costs. In the case of product 1 this proportion is 80/400, which means that 20% of the total fixed cost is assigned to this product. Similarly, 30% of the fixed cost is allocated to product 2 and 50% to product 3. The results of this allocation, referred to as method (a), are shown in Table 11.2, which suggests that the profit margins are 30% and 16% respectively for the first two products, while product 3 is at break-even.

On the basis of this information, it may be tempting to conclude that product 3 is unprofitable, but in reality it only seems unprofitable because of the convention of fixed-cost allocation. It would be erroneous to conclude from these figures that because product 3 does not generate any profit it could be dropped altogether without detrimental effect on the profiability of the plant, unless the

Table 11.2   Cost and profit allocation – method (a)

Product	Fixed cost	Variable cost	Total cost	Revenue	Profit	Margin (%)
1	200	80	280	400	120	30.0
2	300	120	420	500	80	16.0
3	500	200	700	700	0	0
Total	1000	400	1400	1600	200	12.5

elimination of that product would also eliminate the fixed cost of 500 attributed to it.

However, if no reduction in the total cost would ensue as a result of eliminating product 3, namely if the total fixed cost of 1000 has to be recovered from the product mix, irrespective of the volumes of the individual products, then the revenue of 900 generated by the first two products would not be adequate even to cover the total fixed cost of 1000. This means that eliminating product 3, without saving in the total fixed cost, would inevitably lead to an overall loss of 300. Clearly, the method of allocating the fixed cost in Table 11.2 does not recognize the contribution of product 3 and gives rise to misleading conclusions.

This raises the question of whether the fixed cost can be allocated according to some other formula. Of the many possible ways of doing so, consider the following four methods, which allocate the fixed cost to the individual products in proportion to their:

(a) total cost
(b) revenue
(c) profit
(d) equal fixed cost

We shall now examine the consequences of the four alternatives.

(a) Allocation according to total costs

If the total fixed cost is denoted by F and the allocated fixed cost to product 1 is denoted by F_1, and similarly if the total variable cost of the product mix is denoted by S and the variable cost of product 1 by S_1, then:

the total cost C_1 of product 1 is $\qquad C_1 = F_1 + S_1$

the total cost C of the product mix is $\quad C = F + S$

Allocating the fixed cost according to the total cost means that the ratio F_1 to F is equal to the ratio of C_1 to C, namely

$$\frac{F_1}{F} = \frac{F_1 + S_1}{F + S}$$

or

$$\frac{F+S}{F} = \frac{F_1 + S_1}{F_1}$$

from which it follows that

$$\frac{F_1}{F} = \frac{S_1}{S}$$

Thus, the proportion of the fixed cost allocated to product 1 is the same as the ratio of its variable cost to the total variable cost, and similar results are evidently true for the other products. This means that the result of allocating the fixed cost according to proportions of total costs is the same as that performed according variable costs, namely as shown in Table 11.2.

(b) Allocation in proportion to revenues

According to this method, the proportion of the fixed cost allocated to product 1 is given by the ratio of 400 (the revenue of product 1) to 1600 (the total revenue), namely 25%, and similarly 31.2% and 43.8% are allocated to products 2 and 3 respectively. The results,

Table 11.3   Cost and profit allocation – method (b)

Product	Fixed cost	Variable cost	Total cost	Revenue	Profit	Margin (%)
1	250	80	330	400	70	17.5
2	312.5	120	432.5	500	67.5	13.5
3	437.5	200	637.5	700	62.5	8.9
Total	1000	400	1400	1600	200	12.5

Table 11.4   Cost and profit allocation – method (c)

Product	Fixed cost	Variable cost	Total cost	Revenue	Profit	Margin (%)
1	266.7	80	346.7	400	53.3	13.3
2	316.7	120	436.7	500	63.3	12.7
3	416.7	200	616.7	700	83.3	11.9
Total	1000	400	1400	1600	200	12.5

shown in Table 11.3, reveal that product 1 continues to yield the highest profit margin, but it is not as profitable as the figures suggest in Table 11.2. Furthermore, product 3, which just breaks even in Table 11.2, is now profitable, though not as much as the other two products.

(c) Allocation in proportion to profit

If we denote the revenue and total cost of the plant as R and C respectively, then the total profit Z is simply derived as

$$Z = R - C$$

or

$$Z = R - F - S$$

Similarly, for product 1 the profit is

$$Z_1 = R_1 - F_1 - S_1$$

Allocation of the fixed cost according to profit means that

$$\frac{F_1}{F} = \frac{R_1 - F_1 - S_1}{R - F - S}$$

from which it is simple to show that

$$\frac{F_1}{F} = \frac{R_1 - S_1}{R - S}$$

that is, the proportion of the fixed cost allocated to product 1 is the same as the ratio of its so-called direct profit (namely, revenue less variable cost) to the total direct profit. If the values from Table 11.1 are substituted into the last equation, we get

$$\frac{F_1}{1000} = \frac{400 - 80}{1600 - 400}$$

from which the fixed cost allocated to produce 1 is found as

119

Table 11.5 Cost and profit allocation – method (d)

Product	Fixed cost	Variable cost	Total cost	Revenue	Profit	Margin (%)
1	333.3	80	413.3	400	−13.3	−3.3
2	333.3	120	453.3	500	46.7	9.3
3	333.3	200	533.3	700	166.7	23.8
Total	1000	400	1400	1600	200	12.5

$F_1 = 266.7$. Similarly, the fixed cost allocated to the other two products can be computed and the results are as presented in Table 11.4.

(d) Equal allocation of fixed cost

Allocating the same fixed cost to all the products (following the maxim of equal misery for all) ignores the sales volume and the variable cost incurred in the production and processing of each of the products and just takes account of the number of products in the product mix. In our example there are three products and this method would therefore allocate 333.3 as the fixed cost to each, resulting in the cost and profit shown in Table 11.5.

Comparison of the results

A summary of the results of the four allocation methods is given in Table 11.6, from which it transpires that while the ranking of the products in terms of net profit margins remains unchanged for the first three, their perceived profitability greatly depends on which of the methods is adopted. Method (d) even reverses the profitability ranking and product 1, which appears to be the most profitable according to the first three methods, incurs a loss according to the fourth, whereas product 3 is regarded as unprofitable according to method (a) but as the most profitable according to method (d).

Notice that both the net and gross margins for the total product mix remain unchanged throughout at 12.5% and 80% respectively. It is only the internal distribution of the margins between the products that is affected by whatever method is adopted for allocating the total fixed costs.

Clearly, the four allocation methods referred to above do not constitute an exhaustive list and other allocation methods can easily be devised (for example, in proportion to physical volumes, to processing times, to the number of direct employees associated with each of the products, and so on). The degree to which the net profit margin obtained for product 1 depends on the fixed-cost allocation is shown in Figure 11.1: the higher the allocated fixed costs, the lower the profit margin; and similar results may be derived for the other products. The figures in Table 11.6 and Figure 11.1 show the wide variations in possible outcomes, depending on which allocation method is adopted.

What emerges from this example is that analysis cannot be carried out in a vacuum and cannot be divorced from the assumptions made. The structure and implications of a cost and profitability model can only be understood against the framework of these

Table 11.6 Results of four allocation methods

Method	Fixed cost (%)				Net profit margin (%)				Gross margin (%)
	(a)	(b)	(c)	(d)	(a)	(b)	(c)	(d)	
Product									
1	20.0	25.0	26.7	33.3	30.0	17.5	13.3	−3.3	80.0
2	30.0	31.2	31.7	33.3	16.0	13.5	12.7	9.3	76.0
3	50.0	43.8	41.7	33.3	0	8.9	11.9	23.8	71.4
Total	100	100	100	100	12.5	12.5	12.5	12.5	75.0

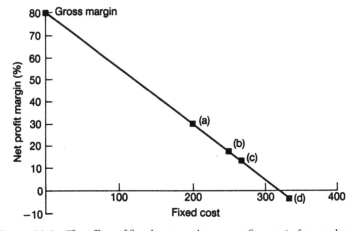

Figure 11.1 The effect of fixed cost on the net profit margin for product 1

assumptions and by taking into account the purpose of the analysis. Thus, the first lesson to be learnt is that assumptions relate not only to the manner in which data are collected (in the above discussion we accepted the raw data in Table 11.1, though questions may well be raised about the procedures used for assembling the basic figures shown), but also to their possible interpretation.

The four methods of fixed-cost allocation suggest different assumptions about the way in which the products in the product mix and their costs are interdependent. For example, it is generally assumed that fixed and variable costs are independent of each other, also that the total cost of any one product is not affected by a change in the total cost of another; however, if the direct cost of product 1 in the above example is reduced, the effect would be to increase the fixed cost assigned to product 3 under method (a), whereas under method (b) it would be unaffected.

Similarly, an increase in revenue for one product would affect the fixed cost, and thereby the total cost, of each of the other products under method (b) but not under the other methods. In contrast, the allocation according to method (d) is immune from all such changes, but the fact that the allocated fixed cost is totally independent of the level of activity or resources related to each of the products casts doubt on the rationale of this method, and it is hardly surprising that it does not have ardent followers in practice.

All this suggests that the allocation methods discussed above cannot be considered as alternative 'causal models'; in other words, they do not provide an 'explanation' by suggesting that a change in variable cost or in revenue *causes* a change in the fixed cost of any particular product. They merely serve as alternative convenient formulae for internal accounting purposes and reveal little about the absolute profitability of individual products.

Conclusion

Perhaps the most important lesson from the above discussion is that the convention for ascertaining cost data cannot be divorced from the purpose of the analysis. If management seeks to rank the products in Table 11.1 in terms of their profitability (measured either by the level of profit or by the net profit margin), then no definitive answer is available, since the level of profitability depends on how the overhead costs are distributed.

Presumably, the quest for information on the individual profit margins stems from a desire to consider whether action can be taken to increase the overall profitability of the product mix, for example by increasing the volume of the most profitable product at the expense of the least profitable, or by replacing the latter with a new product. If *that* is the purpose of the exercise, and if the total fixed cost remains unaffected by changes in the product mix, then clearly the overall profit can be increased when the total direct revenue is increased. In that case, the allocation of fixed cost becomes quite irrelevant. In order to determine how the direct revenue can be increased, further data need to be collected, on the capacity requirements per unit of output of each product and on the scope for changing pricing policies, so that trade-off functions between products can then be established, thereby indicating the desirability or otherwise of product substitution.

Because of the almost arbitrary effect of the fixed-cost allocation on the net profit margin, many analysts prefer to ignore it altogether and assess product profitability by the gross profit margin, which is computed as the ratio of the direct profit (i.e. revenue less marginal cost) to the revenue. The result, shown in the last column of Table 11.6, is not dependent on the allocation method. Changes in revenues and direct costs are clearly reflected in the values of the gross margins, but the disadvantage of relying solely on this criterion is that, by ignoring the fixed cost altogether, it cannot alert management to deterioration in profitability when overhead costs rise. To that end management needs to continue to monitor the overall net profit margin for the product mix. This compromise, of using the gross margin for evaluating individual product profitability and the net margin for the plant as a whole, attempts to make the most of the basic data (such as that shown in Table 11.1), thereby avoiding the most blatant effects of arbitrary cost allocation.

All this may seem obvious enough, and yet we find only too often that when analysts are supplied with financial data, such as in Table 11.2, they tend to proceed on the premiss that the data are value-free and valid for any modelling exercise that may be contemplated. The example discussed in this chapter questions this premiss. Data are rarely absolute; they are the outcome of measurement and recording procedures, which are themselves based on a set of assumptions, hypotheses and beliefs. No modelling exercise is complete without a thorough examination of the origin of the data and without a full understanding of their impact.

In this chapter we analysed the problem of allocating fixed overhead costs. A similar problem occurs in determining transfer prices between different parts of an organization, as highlighted in a little episode recounted in the next chapter, where the issue of allocating overheads is discussed further.

CHAPTER 12

A transfer pricing saga

The hot issue

It was late in the afternoon, after a frustrating and exhausting board meeting. The agenda was not particularly long, and the chairman at first went breezily through the routine items without provoking too much discussion. Then he paused to ascertain whether there were any reactions to a schedule of capital expenditure proposals, but these were all approved, almost on the nod. The next item, dealing with senior staff appointments in the company, was hardly contentious either, only a couple of observations were expressed about the need for developing a more systematic approach to salary grading, in order to attain a reasonable degree of comparability and consistency. Then the chairman moved to the item dealing with company performance, and all hell was let loose.

It was obvious that the board was very concerned about the financial results of two divisions and each of the directors in charge, Abe and Bob, naturally did his best to defend his empire. As the discussion became more and more acrimonious, it became clear that the disenchantment of their fellow directors with the performance of the two divisions had been mounting for some time, and that the familiar excuses of Abe and Bob (which had been offered on numerous past occasions) only served to irritate their listeners and generate further criticisms. It was not long before the two defendants started, in desperation, to blame each other and 'the system' for the alleged shortcomings in performance. After a long and inconclusive debate it was agreed that a small group would convene after the board meeting to discuss the outstanding issues and attempt to resolve them. The group consisted of Charles (the chairman), Abe and Bob, Fin (the finance director), Sue (the sales director) and Mandy (the administration director, also responsible for the personnel function).

Before listening in on their deliberations, it would help us to have a brief and simplified description of how the two divisions operate. Abe's division essentially produces one product, called product A; some of the output is supplied as an input to Bob's division and the balance is sold in the open market. Bob's division uses some other materials purchased from the outside to convert the input A into product B, which is then sold to external customers. The two divisions are treated as separate profit centres and are charged for central overheads in proportion to their respective sales revenues. This is quite a common method of allocating central costs and some of its implications were discussed in the previous chapter.

Charles consulted his watch. It was late in the afternoon, but perhaps a bit too early to offer his colleagues a drink; besides, that might encourage them to prolong the discussions. He was anxious to elicit from them their perceptions of the problems and their proposed remedies, and naturally he asked them to be frank and forthcoming. What follows is a condensed version of their responses, but essentially it is an accurate account of what went on.

The protagonists

Abe: Our main problem stems from the current method of fixing the transfer price charged to my division. I am required to sell to Bob any amount of product A that he specifies at 5% above my average unit cost (which includes all the costs incurred by the division, as well as the central overhead charge), whereas the average selling price that I can achieve in the open market is about 15% above my unit cost. Since my division is treated as an independent profit centre, it would obviously be advantageous to us to sell more outside and less to Bob.

The present system is particularly unfair, because whenever the market price for product A falls below the transfer price, Bob buys from the market and I am then obliged to off-load more of my output on the market, and that depresses the price even further, so that a loss under these circumstances becomes inevitable. Now, the performance of the division is not as good as it should be for two reasons. First, there is uncertainty as to what volume Bob wants me to supply in any period, and as I am prevented from making large production commitments to outside customers, I end up working well below the available capacity; secondly, while I can sell outside more than I do at present, by reducing the selling price and thereby improving my plant utilization, my overall revenue would then deteriorate.

I am also very unhappy about the allocation of the central overheads, over which I do not have any control. Last month I was charged more than the previous month, although my sales revenue actually declined, and the reason for the increased charge was due to some extra expenditure at head office that had nothing to do with the division.

Bob: I must stress two points: first, product A is a vital input to my division and we must therefore be assured of supply, otherwise our plant utilization and revenue, as well as profit, will badly suffer; secondly, as Abe says, product A is available on the open market and as its price fluctuates, I can often buy from other suppliers below our transfer price level. I am willing to accept a reasonable penalty as an insurance for security of supply, and this is why our policy is to continue purchasing from Abe as long as the transfer price does not exceed the market price by more than 5%.

But when the margin is wider, I cannot afford to continue paying too dearly for my inputs and I must then turn to other suppliers; otherwise, my division would become quite uncompetitive with respect to the price that can be obtained for product B. Now, there are occasions when the market price is above Abe's transfer price, and the supply from his division is then vital to protect us from having to go to the market in times of shortage and having to pay inflated prices. If we could not rely on supply from

Abe, these shortages could sometimes badly affect our plant utilization, and hence our financial performance.

It therefore follows that I must retain first call on Abe's output and be absolutely certain of getting my supply from his division whenever I want it. By agreeing to pay him the transfer price even when it exceeds the market price by up to 5%, Abe's division is getting a distinct benefit. The fact that from time to time Abe's unit cost exceeds the market price for product A leads me to believe that his division perhaps lags behind its competitors in efficiency.

As to the allocation of central overheads, it should be appreciated that as the selling price of product B is much higher than that of A, and as the allocation is proportional to revenue, the charge levied on my division is much higher for the same level of physical output than the corresponding charge for Abe's division. This means that we have to absorb a comparatively larger proportion of the central overhead cost, and this factor has an adverse effect on our total cost and on profitability. Incidentally, does Abe realize that if the transfer price were to be increased, his revenue would increase and then his allocation of the central cost would also increase? Surely, from that point of view it would not be in his interest to increase the transfer price.

Sue: Both divisions are not working at full capacity and we could greatly improve our market share if they produced more. I agree with Abe that he should reduce the price to outsiders in order to increase the volume sold. But to make Bob more competitive, we should give consideration to reducing the transfer price, rather than increasing it. By reducing the cost to Bob, the price for product B could be reduced as well, and the allocation of central overheads per unit will also decline, adding further strength to the competitive position of Bob's division. As a result, the sales volume of product B, which generally brings in a far higher revenue than product A, will rise and so will our market share.

Fin: From the overall company viewpoint, it does not make any difference whether the profit per unit of product B is made in one division or the other. They both feed into the same pocket. Similarly, the total central overhead cost for the two divisions is fixed for any given level of total sales revenue, so that a reduction in the allocation to one division merely increases the allocation to the other. We have to distinguish between actions that affect our internal procedures and those that are intended for the market-place. The former are no more than accounting conventions that distribute costs and revenues between operating units, while the latter may affect the total revenue and thereby our overall profitability. In this respect the internal accounting process is a zero sum game, which has no effect on corporate profitability. We seem to be spending an inordinate amount of time on the former, whereas we should concentrate our efforts on improving overall profitability.

One way of eliminating the interminable internal bickering on procedures is to amalgamate the two divisions under one head as a single profit centre, and then the transfer price would not matter. A merged division would also give us an opportunity to examine the question of modernizing the whole production process through the introduction of new technology, whereas at present we have to deal with this kind of capital expenditure on a piecemeal basis.

Mandy: We did have a single division in the past and it did not work. It was simply too big and individual sections within the division felt isolated and had no sense of identity. There was then a distinct lack of incentive. The creation of the two divisions in the form of separate profit centres was meant to introduce this incentive, so that the performance of each division could be judged on its own and could be shown to be viable in comparison with another plant in the industry.

Furthermore, to emphasize the incentive element we agreed to introduce a profit-sharing scheme into the divisions and the question of the transfer price then becomes quite crucial because of its effect on the individual profitability of the divisions. We must undertake a detailed study to review the current transfer price, so that what we come up with is seen to be fair; otherwise, the proposed profit-sharing scheme may well backfire. My suggestion is that we should aim to fix the transfer price in each period at such a level that the resultant average profit share per employee is the same in the two divisions. In this way, we shall avoid jealousy and internal strife.

Charles: As usual, you all made very good points. You all seem to agree that the transfer price is an important issue, but you differ in your suggestions on how to deal with the problem. Abe wants the price to increase, Bob wants it to remain as it is, Sue suggests that it should be reduced, Fin wants to eliminate the problem altogether by merging the divisions, while Mandy argues that we need to review the price to provide an equal incentive for all. So, where do we go from here?

Where indeed? This is not an apocryphal story, although it is told with sparse detail, encapsulating several hours of discussion into a few paragraphs. It is also a story that could be told without an ending, because there are many ways in which the chairman could tackle this problem. In fact, in this case he chose to seek a compromise of a slight adjustment to the transfer price in order to placate his colleagues for a while, until he could get round to a reorganization of the company, with both Abe and Bob being moved to new positions. His judgement was that the friction between the two divisions was entirely due to the strong personalities of their directors.

He confided in his personal assistant by quoting a saying attributed to Dr Robb Wilmot, the previous chairman of the computer company ICL, namely: 'It is people who produce success or cause failure. If you have a problem with the system, then the problem is with the managers. To solve it, change the managers, who will then fix the system.' What Charles failed to appreciate is that the complaints voiced by Abe and Bob were rooted in the system itself and in its procedures, both in the performance evaluation of the divisions as well as in the effect that the profit-sharing scheme had on remuneration to individuals. All this suggests that new divisional heads would soon be subjected to the same stresses experienced by their predecessors and that consequently they would become just as frustrated and just as obstreperous. The central role of transfer pricing in this case is self-evident, and we shall discuss it in greater detail and in conjunction with the concept of accountability in the next chapter.

Questions that the chairman did not ask

What is perhaps significant about this story is that the chairman failed to analyse the arguments of his colleagues and subject them to a critical scrutiny. For example, he could have asked the following questions:

(a) Since the central overheads costs are indeed outside the control of the divisional heads, should consideration be given to abolishing their allocation to the divisions? Many companies do, in fact, designate their head office as a separate cost centre and do not attempt to allocate its costs to profit centres in the organization. If information on unit cost and profitability does not have to be presented to a third party, then divisional accounts are often prepared solely for internal management accounting purposes, and under such circumstances there may be no need to allocate central overhead costs to operating divisions. However, when price negotiations with a third party are heavily dependent on disclosure of detailed costs (as is the case, for example, in some government contracts), a formula for allocating central overheads has to be agreed by those concerned.

(b) Why does Abe get to know Bob's requirements for product A so late in the day that he does not know what level of production capacity to commit to outside sales? Analysis of past requirements may well reveal that there is a base level that may be regarded as certain and which Abe can count on. Over and above that level there may be an additional requirement that Bob can identify at short notice; whether he should then be able to expect emergency supplies from Abe or have to buy in the market is an open question.

(c) Why should Bob be given complete freedom to decide

131

whether to buy from Abe or from other suppliers, whereas Abe is not allowed a similar choice as to whether he should sell to Bob or not? The current system is clearly designed to ensure that Bob gets his supply at almost the lowest market price or almost the lowest production cost, whichever is the lower. However, at times when the market price is high, he gets a distinct advantage over his competitors at the expense of Abe's division. Is this in the best interest of the organization as a whole?

(d) What is the justification in Mandy's proposal for fixing the transfer price at a level that will result in equal profit share for all? If everyone is to get the same benefit, where is the divisional and individual incentive? If the purpose of the profit-sharing scheme is to encourage the employees to think not only about their own division, but become identified with the organization as a whole, would it not be preferable to link the scheme to the overall performance of the company, so that it becomes independent of the transfer price?

(e) If, as discussed above, Bob needs to be assured of supply from Abe, and if Abe is to be assured of demand from Bob, by committing both divisions to a specified quantity during any given period, would not the simplest method of fixing the transfer price be to equate it with the average market price during that period? In this way, neither division can be said to take undue advantage of the other, since the alternative sources of supply for Bob and the alternative customers of Abe would be subjected to the same price.

The need for a searching analysis

One can go on and ask further questions to expose the self-interest of the various protagonists and the weaknesses in their respective arguments. Because the existing procedures and their consequences are not merely financial, but embedded in the internal power structure, it is difficult to point to a single, let alone an 'optimal', solution. And, in any event, what is the meaning of a 'solution' in these circumstances? If, as a result of changing the transfer price, Abe's division does better while Bob's is worse off, is that a 'solution', or is it just an interim state that redefines the problem in search of a new 'solution'?

What is perhaps both baffling and depressing in this episode was that the possible contribution of management science to the resolution of the problem was not even considered. The chairman could have commissioned a study that would try first to establish both the corporate and divisional objectives and constraints; secondly, trace the behaviour of the market over time in terms of overall sales and prices; and thirdly, build a model to determine the consequences to the divisions and to the company of alternative procedures and decisions.

One cannot guarantee that such a study would have necessarily resolved all the inter-divisional problems and that the internal power struggle would then have subsided. But at least the chairman would have developed a better understanding of the various ramifications and the modelling exercise could have helped him to control the organization more decisively, and perhaps more wisely, than hitherto.

CHAPTER 13

Divide and rule

The organization chart

We have seen examples in earlier chapters of how management philosophies and managerial perceptions of contraints and opportunities can have a profound influence on corporate performance. These philosophies often find expression in the way the enterprise is organized and in the design of lines of demarcation of authority, accountability and responsibility.

'Accountability' has become the watchword in the assessment of corporate performance in relation to organizational design. When management consultants are called in by senior executives to evaluate the organizational structure of an enterprise, one of the key questions that they are asked is whether the demarcation of tasks and responsibilities of subsidiaries, departments and managers is logical and appropriate, or whether a new grouping of activities would be more conducive to achieving the overall aims of the chief executive and the board.

In a sense, the organization structure is a manifestation of an allocation of resources in order to perform an array of tasks, broadly defined as production, marketing and distribution of given products and services. The first stage of this allocation exercise takes the form of an organization chart, which shows the groupings and their reporting relationships within the structure. An overall chart outlines the position of subsidiaries, divisions and departments, while more detailed charts highlight the relationships between sections and individuals.

Reporting relationships automatically define assigned responsibilities, although – largely for the sake of simplicity – charts concentrate on unidimensional vertical relationships and tend to gloss over the more complicated communications network with staff functions and with peers located in other parts of the organization. It has often been said that for successful coordination, effective feedback and speed of response, the non-vertical relationships, and particularly those of the informal variety, are far more important than the vertical ones, but these are difficult to incorporate in an organization chart and are therefore often implied, or allowed to evolve.

The organization chart needs to be followed by a schedule of objectives and bench-marks for each of the entities in the structure. As already indicated in other chapters, the assumption is that the overall objectives of the enterprise can be disaggregated into sub-objectives and can be assigned to specific units in the form of targets for production levels, sales revenues and costs. The sub-objectives for each of the entities in the organization structure are translated into a budget plan, with a corresponding allocation of resources, and targets are set for revenue, cost, profit, and various specified performance ratios (such as cost or revenue proportions, profit margins, and return on investment). Targets often indicate the acceptable performance levels expected from a particular unit, and actual performance, which achieves these targets or improves on them, is usually rewarded by financial and other incentives, and also by better promotion prospects for individuals.

The emergence of accountability

The rationale for this system is simple enough (Eilon 1979a):

- in order to complete an array of tasks and to achieve specified goals, there is a need to determine group and individual responsibilities
- responsibility is defined by tasks, allocated resources, performance objectives, and reporting relationships
- assigned individual responsibility automatically implies account-ability to a higher authority for one's actions and performance
- the management control process consists of feedback information and taking corrective action
- incentive schemes are designed to encourage groups and individuals to achieve the desired performance levels.

Thus, the cornerstone of this management philosophy is *account-ability*, and this is why management consultants are eager to ensure that the process described above is rigorously applied to every subsidiary, every division and every department in the organization. Implementation of this scheme provides senior executives with information about which entities perform well, which perform only adequately, and which fall below the mark, and this information focuses attention on measures that need to be undertaken to improve results.

I have heard the ugly term 'every tub on its own bottom' used to describe the essence of this philosophy: every entity is considered a profit centre and has to show a positive bottom-line result to justify its continued existence. If an entity does not perform satisfactorily, it should be reorganized, or its management should be replaced, and if there are no prospects for future improvement, then the entity should be disposed of. The maxim of 'divide and rule', so it is argued, provides senior executives with an effective management control process, aiming to ensure that every part of the structure makes a positive contribution to the wellbeing of the enterprise. The performance of each unit can be evaluated by comparison with past performance, with the planned budget, or with other units (in the organization or elsewhere), and the results can be used for future planning exercises and for strategic realignment.

All this sounds simple and logical enough, provided the profit centres defined in the structure are self-contained and sell their physical products or services direct to the market. But what do you do when a particular entity does not generate profit from the market-place and is strictly a cost centre and not a profit centre? Effectively, then, financial control is confined to judging its expenses against budget.

This is not entirely satisfactory for two reasons. First, the very basis for allocating a budget to a cost centre may be open to question, often because of its arbitrary nature or because it merely perpetuates past practices (as we saw in the last two chapters). Secondly, and more importantly, a systematic performance evaluation can only make sense when outputs are judged against inputs. If an operating entity sells to the market, the outputs may be measured by the sales revenue and the inputs by the cost incurred. But if there is no sales revenue, we are left with one side of the equation only, namely with the inputs, and consequently the evaluation becomes inadequate.

Transfer pricing

The solution to this problem, proposed by the proponents of 'every tub on its own bottom', is to convert all cost centres into profit centres. The argument goes something like this: if department (or plant) A supplies its products or services to another department, B, then A should be credited with the value of the supplied products and services while B should be similarly debited. In short, a system of transfer pricing needs to be implemented for the value of A's output to be ascertained, and if this system applies throughout the organization, then every entity, whether it is self-contained or not, would be on the same footing.

If, for example, department A sells some of its output to the market and supplies the rest to other parts of the organization (this is the case discussed in the previous chapter), then its total output is simply the sum of the external sales revenue and the 'internal revenue', the latter being determined by the transfer-pricing mechanism. Similarly, the total cost of any given department consists of all its direct costs, including products and services bought from the outside, plus all those 'bought' from other departments. In this way, the 'profit' of the department is obtained as the difference between its total 'revenue' and total 'cost', and the total profit of the enterprise is the sum of the 'profits' of the individual parts. Simple, isn't it?

Simple and adequate it is for most purposes. But, in addition to some notable and important exceptions, there are many problems of implementation, as we have already seen in the previous chapter and as the following examples demonstrate.

Case 1: Product portfolio

Take the case of two independent divisions, A and B, both self-contained. They neither receive any inputs from nor supply outputs to other parts of the organization (i.e. both sell their entire outputs to the market). Each is fully accountable for its actions and performance.

Their products are not in competition, but complement each other in the market, constituting a kind of product portfolio, they enjoy a good reputation in the industry and have many customers in common. On the face of it, this is a simple case for the application of the profit centre concept.

Now, division A is profitable, while division B is not, and all attempts to improve the performance of B have failed. The fact that B is losing money dilutes the earnings of the total enterprise and depresses its share price. What is the chief executive to do about this state of affairs?

Now, the doctrine of complete accountability dictates that, if there is no prospect for B to improve, the division should be disposed of or closed down. However, such action would ignore the negative reactions of customers, whose needs are supplied from both divisions. If B is acquired by another corporation, or if B closes down, customers would have to go elsewhere for their type-B products and – in due course – may also shift their demand for type-A products to another supplier. As a result, the total sales volume of division A would fall, and so would its profitability.

The product portfolio implies that while in this example the divisions A and B are entirely independent entities, *their products are not*. Here the very presence of B in the market supports the sales of A's output. Strictly, this fact should be reflected in the accounts by a debit to A and a credit to B (i.e. a kind of a transfer credit) for this market support. However, in practice it would be difficult for the protagonists to forecast what would happen to A's profitability if B were to be eliminated, and hence difficult to determine the appropriate transfer credit. In such a case, management would have to concede that the financial performance of the parts does not reveal the full story about the performance of the whole.

Case 2: Dual-destination output

Suppose department A supplies both the market and department B (as in the example in the previous chapter). In negotiating the transfer price, A naturally wishes to be credited with the price at which it sells to the market. But B may argue for a lower price on the following grounds:

138

- In supplying the market, A has to carry expenses for advertising, selling and distribution. Most of these costs are not incurred when supplying B, hence some of the saving should be passed on to B in the form of a discount, resulting in a lower transfer price.
- As a long-term customer for A's output (perhaps unlike other customers in the market), B deserves a special discount for contributing a measure of stability and continuity to A's production schedules (see the example in the previous chapter).
- In supplying the market, A incurs fixed costs, which do not grow in proportion to output volume. The cost per unit supplied to B is, therefore, lower than the cost per unit supplied to the market, and this should be reflected in the transfer price.
- B can find an alternative source in the market at a lower price than the transfer price, and demands that the lower price should therefore apply.

To avoid many of these and allied problems, senior executives often decree that the transfer-pricing formula should be based on an arm's-length relationship. This means that B is free to seek quotations from any potential supplier and to select the one that offers the best value in terms of quality, delivery and price. If, for strategic considerations, the chief executive wishes to maintain A as the supplier to B, then the transfer price is fixed at the level of the best quotation.

This procedure is thought to be fair to both sides: B is not penalized for using an internal source, while A has to face the harsh reality of competition and take action to ensure that its profitability is not unduly eroded by the agreed transfer price. In the event that A is unwilling to supply B at the proposed price, then B is free to be served by an external supplier. This arm's-length relationship ensures that market forces and freedom of action reiterate the concept of accountability.

It should be appreciated, however, that this solution may, in turn, lead to other problems: if the procedures outlined above become known to outside suppliers, some may feel that they are merely being used as a pawn in the power game between A and B and refuse to quote. Others may quote artificially low prices in order to remove the stranglehold that A has over B, in the hope of winning the order and disrupting both the cost structure and the profitability of A's operations.

The fact that B is better off in the short term, by buying from an external supplier at a lower quotation than A's, may not necessarily be good for the enterprise as a whole, and indeed may not be in B's long-term interests either, if ensuring dependability of supply at a low price is regarded as an important criterion. It is also possible that by allowing the external supplier to win an order from B against the competition from A, the supplier's total output volume would rise. He would then enjoy the growing benefits of economies of scale, become more profitable, and constitute a greater threat to A's future. To allow B a completely free hand, without any regard to the long-term consequences for A, could therefore be distinctly damaging to the enterprise, and ironically it would be the fault of its own management for creating the conditions for the competitor to succeed.

Case 3: Management services

The above case is concerned with a department which supplies the external market as well as other departments within the enterprise. There are departments, however, that do not generate any revenue from external sales and are solely concerned with providing internal services to other parts of the organization. A department of management services is a notable example.

The doctrine of transfer pricing requires that the services are 'charged' to 'customer departments'. The cross-charging of the management services department can follow one of two methods. The first takes the form of a head-office decision as to how the cost (or budget) of the department should be allocated which may be in proportion to sales revenues of operating divisions, or the numbers of their employees, or according to some other easily applied criteria (some of which were discussed in Chapter 11).

This method, which should properly be called 'transfer costing' rather than 'transfer pricing', takes no account of the wishes or preferences of the 'customers', who are charged the same amount irrespective of how much or how frequently they avail themselves of the services on offer. It is not difficult to see that such an approach soon breeds resentment, since managers do not like being charged for services they have not requested. In fact, this method has no advantage over the more simplistic concept of a cost centre and, although it is often employed in practice by many financial controllers, there seems little merit in adopting this method of cost allocation.

The second method requires the department to record the services provided in terms of the resources used, such as manpower, materials and computing time, and then charge the customer departments accordingly. Usually, the charging rates reflect either the actual 'costs incurred' or quoted market rates that would have applied had the services been provided by an external agency. In either case, the purpose of the exercise is not to encourage the management services department to produce a profit, but to prove that its services are really wanted and that its costs are accounted for and are absorbed by the operating divisions.

As pointed out elsewhere (Eilon 1979b), apart from responding to specific needs of 'client departments', the prime function of management services, and not least of an OR (Operational Research) department, is to assist head office in the task of the overall direction of the enterprise, by collating and analysing information in various key areas (such as the use of financial and manpower resources, production operations, sales and marketing, distribution and logistics, targeting and corporate performance) in order to propose ways for improvement.

Furthermore, if the initiation of studies to evaluate the performance of their activities is left entirely to the discretion of operating people, there is a real risk that many potentially valuable projects would never be commissioned. The fact remains that many operators take a very narrow view of what their problems and interests are, and there is therefore a need to create the conditions for objective studies to be undertaken, setting aside vested interests and cutting across departmental boundaries (Eilon 1979b: 177).

These arguments have long led me to conclude that the principle of charging for management services is misguided, that particularly in the case of OR it tends to encourage work of a tactical nature, that it makes the analysts identify too closely with the clients who commission the work and who foot the bill, and that it rarely allows important and innovative projects to be started without the explicit request of paying sponsors (Eilon 1985: 38). There is, therefore, a need for a central interventionist policy to be robustly applied in order to ensure that projects are undertaken, even in the absence of the so-called clients' appproval. My many encounters with top managers and with management services and OR departments over the years have served to reinforce my convictions in this regard.

Case 4: Computing and management information systems

Another example, in some ways similar to that of management services, is that of computing and IT (Information Technology). In spite of recent trends in many companies for departments to rely increasingly on local microcomputers rather than on a remote mainframe machine, the importance of an all-embracing MIS (Management Information System) is still very much in evidence. The need for reliable and up-to-date information being instantly available at many points of inquiry throughout the organization means that elaborate communications, storage and retrieval systems have to be written and maintained by a central authority. There are many enterprises where MIS represents the basic fabric of the managerial process and all those connected to the system are locked in and just cannot 'opt out', as the organization becomes heavily dependent on computer mainframe facilities.

A good example is the branch network of a bank, or the outlets of a multiple chain store, where each branch or outlet is connected to the central computer, both for updating financial transactions and for information retrieval purposes. The branches or outlets have no choice in the matter; they have to be connected, because the very essence of their operations is dictated by the MIS framework. How then should the costs of the central facility be allocated to the branches?

One possible answer is to allocate the central costs in proportion to the branch size (revenue, manpower, direct costs) or its operations (number of transactions, number of computer inquiries). But if the branch manager has no choice on whether to be connected to the computer system or not, the charge becomes an uncontrollable overhead (i.e. uncontrollable by the user), like the cost of premises, and this distorts the financial performance of the branch personnel. Whether the cost of the central computer facility is allocated or remains a part of a central cost centre is, therefore, not a question of principle, but one of dubious administrative convenience.

Even when a manager does have a choice of whether to use the central computer or not, the question of transfer pricing is far from simple, as suggested by the following example. An engineering company with a complex product range has excellent central computing facilities and a widespread network of terminals to many locked-in users (mainly engaged in design, materials specifications, procurement and inventory control), who are charged according to a simple formula, based primarily on usage of CPU (Central Processing Unit) time. The manufacturing director wants to introduce a computerized production-scheduling system, which can be loaded either on the central mainframe or on an external computer bureau. Before deciding which option to take, he asks the computer department and the external bureau for price quotations.

The computer department is working at 63% utilization and its manager estimates that the requirements of the new production-scheduling system would increase utilization to 75%. He works out the average cost per CPU that would obtain for 75% utilization and proceeds to quote that figure as a transfer price.

The computer manager realizes that if the same rate is then applied to everybody, the current rate for the other users would fall, the computer department would continue to recover its total costs and the manufacturing department would then have to pay 16% of these costs (corresponding to its share of the utilized capacity). It then transpires that his rate is higher than the one quoted by the bureau and that there is a distinct possibility, therefore, that the manufacturing director would opt for the services of the bureau.

Now, as the costs of the computer department (which mainly consists of fixed costs, owing to the heavy capital outlay on hardware and fixed staff) are already fully recovered by the locked-in users, and as the increase in utilization from 63% to 75% would largely involve only additional marginal costs, it is possible to devise a formula that would result in the manufacturing department having to shoulder only 10% (instead of the 16% based on average costing) of the total costs. This would make the internal rate competitive with the bureau's, it would still result in some cost reduction for the other users, but the result would mean differential pricing, since the rate offered to the manufacturing department would be distinctly lower than that imposed on the others. Whether resorting to differential rates, which essentially depend on whether the user is locked in or not, would result in a healthy and acceptable outcome remains an open question. Locked-in users may well feel that they would become the victims of unfair discrimination perpetrated by a centralized monopolistic authority.

Case 5: Other head-office functions

Apart from management services, there are many other head-office functions that constitute a mixture: they both provide services and direct assistance to operating divisions, in the form of information and analysis, and at the same time constitute an integral part of the overall managerial control process. Some are more directly related to operational activities, such as advertising, promotion, marketing and distribution. Others are concerned not just with current operations, but with future disposition of resources, such as financial control, personnel, corporate planning, product design, and R&D. How are their services to be charged to the operating divisions?

The logic of a transfer-pricing formula in these cases can hardly be sustained. Whether the services are explicitly requested by the operators, or whether they are maintained at the behest of the senior executives in the organization, defining the services in terms of outputs, to which prices need to be assigned, would be regarded by many as an artificial and sterile exercise. Consequently, in many organizations such activities are left as cost centres without attempts to allocate their costs.

In others, the pressure for accountability is so intense that the central functions are broken up and many of their activities are divested to the operating divisions. Thus, an operating division would have its own personnel department, its own sales and marketing, its own financial control, even its own R&D. The rationale for this arrangement stems from the desire to enforce the principle of accountability, in that decisions on expenditure in each of these functions are then in the hands of the executive in charge of the division. He (she) can increase or decrease expenditure as he sees fit, and that would be reflected in his bottom line. At the end of the day, he remains responsible and accountable for his decisions and actions, and in this way the organization avoids unnecessary and costly proliferation at the centre.

The result is a lean head office, concentrating only on central planning and control, operating almost like a holding company, while all the operators constitute independent subsidiaries. There are many advantages to such an arrangement (as discussed briefly in Chapter 3). First and foremost, it does not impose on operators overhead costs which are totally outside their control. Secondly, a lean central office can devote all its efforts to overall direction and strategic planning, rather than get side-tracked by detailed minor issues. Thirdly, an independent and self-contained subsidiary can be more easily disposed of than one which is part of an integrated organization, and this adds to the flexibility of the board in considering future strategy.

The downside is that the management of an operating division would be too concerned with short-term performance and disinclined to invest in long-term prospects. In the case of R&D, for example, the interests of the operating division would generally be confined to a limited time horizon; consequently, it would refrain from exploring areas likely to benefit other divisions or devoting a great deal of manpower and financial resources to speculative innovation. Another example is in the area of personnel, where an operating division may be more reluctant to invest in training and management development on a large scale, and tend to resist vigorously the transfer of good talent to another division.

A second disadvantage is that with each division paddling its own canoe, there is the potential loss of economies of scale and the risk of duplication. For example, if each division has its own computer facility and its own MIS, a great deal of duplication may be involved in developing and maintaining software and hardware systems. If each division is responsible for its own purchasing, the purchasing muscle of the organization may not be fully exploited. If each division is engaged in developing and running its own training courses, the overall cost to the enterprise could be far greater than when these activities are pooled. If each division does its own market research, its own selling, its own promotion and distribution, the focus on the overall needs of the customer may be lost, as well as the opportunity to serve him (or her) more effectively and more efficiently. A further disadvantage is that when a technological or administrative expertise is developed in a division, that expertise would be lost to the enterprise if the division is disposed of.

To overcome these shortcomings, the head office needs to develop and maintain certain facilities, such as a central R&D laboratory, a central treasury function and financial control, manpower planning and management development, public relations and advertising, and so on. The larger the enterprise, the greater is the pressure for these central functions to be maintained at a reasonable level. However, as they grow in scope and size, duplication of activities already performed at the divisional level may grow as well.

The lesson to be learnt from this discourse is that administrative and organizational solutions can always be devised to promote the principle of accountability, but each solution breeds new problems and involves certain penalties. The wide variety of organizational schemes adopted in practice suggests that no solution is eminently superior compared with the alternatives, and that each has its advantages and disadvantages.

Case 6: The head-office nucleus

The extent to which the various head-office support functions, enumerated above, can and should be devolved to independent accountable subsidiaries is, as we have seen, debatable and a matter of judgement. Solutions may depend on the affinity of products covered by the enterprise, on its size and geographical dispersion, on the practices followed by competitors, and above all on the management philosophy of the board.

But there is a nucleus of executives at head office, such as the chief executive, the finance and other functional directors, and their supporting staff, who cannot be transferred to divisions. In addition, there are other central expenses, such as premises, office equipment, travelling, representation, auditors, lawyers, and so on. If they are not incurred directly on behalf of a particular division, they remain as central costs of the head-office nucleus. The general convention is that these costs are not allocated to operating divisions, because they are not incurred at their request and cannot be controlled by them. Such a cost allocation would yield no benefit and only arouse unwelcome criticisms about the level of expenditure at the centre.

Conclusion

The unfettered application of the principle of accountability has many attractions in terms of effective overall control, but it is not without its problems when it comes to implementation. The reason for the difficulties that are encountered in reality stems from the fact that all organizations have intertwined activities and are managed (and served) by common functions, so that accountability has to employ the concept of transfer pricing to allow all inputs and outputs of any given organizational entity to be expressed in monetary terms.

The difficulties fall into three categories. The first concerns the problem of determining prices for products or services supplied internally, where comparisons with market prices are not always relevant, as some of the examples described above illustrate. Not only are there often technical problems in interpreting and analysing cost data, but there is the added problem that a price in an open market signifies the acquiescence of buyer and seller for a transaction to take place, whereas the relationships between an internal supplier and an internal consumer are much more complicated.

Secondly, there are central functions, discussed under case 5, which contribute to the welfare of operating divisions in unquantifiable ways, or in circumstances where the users of a service are locked in and have no discretion regarding the level to which the service is used. Any attempt to allocate costs under these circumstances can only lead to arbitrary decisions, which deny users the freedom to make choices and hence negate the principle of accountability. The extreme example is that described in case 6, which concerns the cost of the head-office nucleus, including the board, the chief executive, the main functional directors, and their supporting staff. Allocating their costs to operating divisions serves no practical purpose.

The third difficulty arises from the fact that transfer pricing concentrates the minds of accountable managers on the short term, and they then tend to ignore, or disregard, the consequences of their actions on other parts of the organization and on the enterprise. We saw how in case 1 a myopic view of accountability can lead to supporting a competitor at the expense of an internal operating division, and how the transfer price in case 4 can be computed in a number of ways that can affect the decision of whether the service is procured internally or externally.

We have to realize that transfer pricing is not a panacea to cure all ills. It helps in the process of *divide and rule*, which has its advantages in creating and promoting effective management control, particularly for large and complex organizations. But claims that it provides an accurate means for determining the profitability or contribution made by each part of the organization are plainly exaggerated; furthermore, they very often tend to ignore the long-term consequences that may ensue.

References

Eilon, S. 1979a. *Management Control*. Oxford: Pergamon Press.
Eilon, S. 1979b. *Aspects of Management*. Oxford: Pergamon Press.
Eilon, S. 1985. *Management Assertions and Aversions*. Oxford: Pergamon Press.

CHAPTER 14

Management performance appraisal

The need for appraisal

The most important resource that an organization has is its employees. Every manager has a responsibility to the organization to make good use of this resource; he (or she) also has a responsibility to the employees under his (or her) control, to guide them, to train and develop them, and last but not least to provide them with information: about the organization, about the business and about their performance. This responsibility is an essential element of the manager's job, and he needs to be trained to do it just as effectively as he is expected to perform all his other managerial duties.

Who decides:
- What activities should an organization undertake?
- What products or services should it produce?
- What markets should it go for?
- What prices should be charged?
- What resources are needed and how should they be utilized?
- What people should be recruited and how should they be compensated?

In short, who carries out the myriad of tasks that keep the organization going and ensures that it is on target?

The answer, of course, is: managers. They are the instrument of planning, decision making and implementation. Without managers, there is no meaning to the organizational structure, no coherent corporate activity, no framework for planning and controlling operations. Of the various resources available to an enterprise, managers are arguably the most important, in that it is they who determine how all the other resources – people, money, materials, plant and machinery – should best be employed to achieve corporate goals.

It is inevitable, as we saw in the previous chapter, that the organization needs to develop a system of accountability in order to assess the performance and progress of various parts of the enterprise. It is equally inevitable that the organization should develop a system for appraising managers in order to address the following simple questions. Do they do a good job? If so, should they be promoted, and if not, what action needs to be taken to improve matters?

Different organizations vary enormously in their approaches to managerial appraisal. At one extreme there are those who pride themselves on having very informal systems, consisting of unstructured and sporadic exchange of views between a few senior members of the hierarchy, involving the absolute minimum of paperwork and feedback to those concerned. In large organizations, such informality has long been regarded as totally inadequate. Instead, the design of sophisticated and highly structured systems has been encouraged, so that appraisal is carried out at regular intervals, usually annually or even more frequently, following a clear set of rules as to who should do the appraising, how the appraisal should be conducted and how those appraised should be involved. In addition, there is a need to specify what is to be done when the appraisal is complete and what actions, if any, need to be undertaken.

Although such elaborate systems tend to be time-consuming and often require a great deal of administration, it is generally recognized that an organization needs to tolerate them nonetheless, at the very least in order to meet various legal requirements in the area of employment. But in the main, appraisal is necessary because the organization wishes to improve its managerial performance, both in the short term, by taking steps to eliminate perceived weaknesses and shortcomings, and in the long term, by instituting training and career development programmes. Appraisal is good management practice to that end.

It is appropriate in this context to mention an interesting article by Douglas McGregor entitled 'An uneasy look at performance appraisal' (1957). Though published over thirty years ago it still makes fascinating reading. He started his article by noting that performance appraisal was on the increase, often as part of management development programmes, adding that the more the method was used, the more uneasy he grew over the assumptions behind it. As he saw it,

> Formal performance appraisal plans are designed to meet three needs, one for the organization and two for the individual: (1) They provide systematic judgements to back up salary increases, promotions, transfers, and sometimes demotions or terminations. (2) They are a means of telling a subordinate how he is doing, and suggesting needed changes in his behavior, attitudes, skills, or job knowledge; they let him know 'where he stands' with the boss. (3) They also are being increasingly used as a basis for the coaching and counseling of the individual by the superior.

Who should do the appraising?

Not all managers like doing the appraising. Some feel distinctly ill at ease in that role, partly because it inevitably involves subjective judgement and possibly personal bias, and partly because they dislike participating in a process likely to affect the welfare of people they know well. Many believe that their responsibility should be confined to their own technical areas of functional expertise (such as production, marketing, finance, R&D); others contend that they lack the necessary skills to assess the performance of their subordinates and are worried about making serious errors. In short, while many managers readily accept that managerial appraisal is important and has to be done, they prefer not to do it themselves. 'Let someone else do it.' That 'someone else' may either be the personnel department ('they designed the assessment system and all the paperwork that goes with it, so let them do it!'), or some external agency, such as consultants specializing in this area.

Both solutions are, however, quite inappropriate. The managerial task encompasses the management of *all* resources, of which people usually constitute the most important element. A relationship between a manager and his (or her) superior is an integral part of their respective jobs, involving their individual aspirations and their expectations of each other. Assessment of performance cannot be divorced from this relationship and cannot, therefore, be delegated to a third party. In the same way that a manager has to be accountable for all his other managerial actions, he has to assume responsibility for assessing subordinates and for the consequences that such an appraisal may entail. Appraisal of managers has to be carried out by their own managers.

McGregor's thesis

In his article McGregor (1957), too, highlights the intense resistance encountered from managers entrusted with the responsibility for carrying out such appraisal schemes, and suggests that this resistance stems from various causes: normal dislike of criticizing subordinates, dislike of new procedures and the way they operate, lack of interviewing skills, and 'mistrust of the validity of the appraisal instrument'. As a consequence, McGregor observes, appraisals are badly conducted and employees get very little feedback, or none at all. Attempts to rectify the situation by providing training programmes in appraisal and interviewing techniques, or by introducing group appraisals (which tend to produce consensus judgement and eliminate extreme views) do not seem, in his view, to have overcome the basic problem of resistance and mistrust. McGregor explains this phenomenon as follows:

> The conventional approach, unless handled with consummate skill and delicacy, constitutes something dangerously close to a violation of the intregrity of the personality. Managers are uncomfortable when they are put in a position of 'playing God'. The respect we hold for the inherent value of the individual leaves us distressed when we must take responsibility for judging the personal worth of a fellow man. Yet the conventional

approach to performance appraisal forces us, not only to make such judgements and to see them acted upon, but also to communicate them to those we have judged. Small wonder we resist!

And he concludes that: 'The modern emphasis upon the manager as a leader who strives to *help* his subordinates achieve both their own and company's objectives is hardly consistent with the judicial role demanded by most appraisal plans.'

McGregor concedes that evaluating subordinates may be necessary for salary and promotion administration, 'but are the subordinates like products on an assembly line, to be accepted or rejected as a result of an inspection process?' It is this concept of product inspection that, in McGregor's view, is the cause of the 'conflict with our convictions about the worth and the dignity of the human personality'; the two are incompatible, 'one or the other must give'. His contention is that 'the organization must yield in the face of this fundamental human value', that it must resolve not to adopt a 'compromise to hide this dilemma', but devise a new approach. He follows Peter Drucker's (1954) concept of 'management by objectives' and argues that the starting point must be for the subordinate 'to establish short-term performance goals *for himself*, assess his own strengths and weaknesses and formulate his own plan for achieving his objectives over a period of, say, six months, after which he should conduct a self-appraisal of what he has achieved. 'The superior's role is to help the man relate his self-appraisal, his 'targets', and his plans for the ensuing period to the realities of the organization' (McGregor 1957). Although the superior has a power of veto ('in an organizational hierarchy anything else would be unacceptable'), McGregor contends that in practice he would rarely need to use it, since 'most subordinates tend to underestimate both their potentialities and achievements'.

The main thrust of this approach, according to McGregor (1957), is that formal appraisal is replaced by what he calls 'analysis', that the subordinate 'becomes an active agent, not a passive "object"', and that he ceases to be 'a pawn in a chess game called management development'. After all, so the argument goes, the subordinate knows best about his own capabilities, shortcomings, needs and objectives, though how this assertion stands up against the earlier statement that he tends to underestimate his potential is less than clear.

Maslowism and Taylorism

What is so intriguing about McGregor's article is the seeming timelessness of the issues raised; in fact, I suspect that if the article had been written today, it would have been received with just as much approbation by social scientists as it was thirty years ago. Admittedly, the 1950s signalled the emergence of some persuasive and seminal writings that came to dominate the management literature for the next three decades, and McGregor's thinking must have been greatly influenced by Maslow, his well-known contemporary ('his is the most fruitful approach I know' (McGregor 1957)).

It was Maslow who wrote extensively on motivation, and he proposed as early as 1954 the concept of a hierarchy of man's needs, namely the notion that as man's aspirations are met, new needs emerge, and this process must continue, eventually culminating in the ultimate desire for what Maslow called 'self-actualization'. It may be argued, therefore, that if you believe in Maslow's proposition that employees should be allowed to develop to their own perceived potential and be given opportunities to achieve both their immediate and ultimate aspirations, then McGregor's views on management appraisal must naturally follow.

It would be a mistake to suppose that the issues aired by Maslow and McGregor were new even during the 1950s. As remarked elsewhere (Eilon 1979, ch. 7), the prime culprit according to the writers at the time (and ever since, for that matter) on management theory and practice has been Taylorism and its mechanistic approach to management control. Taylor preceded McGregor at the beginning of the century by propounding the theory that employees should be given tasks that would suit them best in terms of their performance, and in that sense Taylorism and Maslowism had a common ideal of employing people to the best of their potential.

The main difference between them was that, whereas Taylor was primarily interested in finding the right people to execute given jobs, Maslow's concern was to shape and modify jobs to fit given people. As a consequence, Taylor's prescription was to identify and

154

train what he called 'first class men', selected by reason of aptitude and skill, to perform particular tasks (Taylor 1911), and his obsession with employee efficiency inevitably led to increasing division of labour, increasing specialization, increasing repetitiveness of operations with short cycle times, and increasing boredom on the job; in contrast, the approach of the Maslow school is to start with an understanding of the needs of the employees and then proceed with job enlargement and work design in order to meet the workers' aspirations, and to enhance job satisfaction through motivation.

The contrast between the two schools is rooted in the old problem of how to reconcile the needs of the individual with the needs of the organization, and neither provides a satisfactory answer. Taylor's solution was to staff industry only with 'first class men', arguing that every man (provided he is willing to work) has the aptitude for being best at something. He failed, however, to deal with what I called elsewhere (Eilon 1979: 67) 'Wilson's principle of imbalance' (Wilson was the Chairman of the Special Committee of the House of Representatives to 'Investigate the Taylor and Other Systems of Shop Management', before whom Taylor gave his testimony in 1912).

'Do you mean to tell the committee', Wilson asked Taylor, 'that society is so well balanced that it just provides the proper number of individuals who are fitted to a particular line of work to furnish society with the products of that line of work?' In other words, Wilson postulated (as is clear from this and other persistent questions) that it is too much to expect a balance between supply and demand, namely a complete equilibrium between the kind of jobs that people want to do and the jobs that are available.

Curiously enough, this also turned out to be the fundamental cause for Maslow's failure forty years later in his search for nirvana through self-actualization (as Maslow said, 'What man *can* be, he must be' (1954: 16), but in reality, 'what do you do ... when in a production department everyone wants to be foreman and no one wants to be an operator, or when in an office everyone wants to manage and no one wants to type? ... someone has to to do the manual, mundane, and routine tasks' (Eilon 1979: 69)).

I have dwelt here on the philosophies of Taylorism and Maslowism because they explain the dilemma facing readers of McGregor's article. Although written over thirty years ago, many will argue that his message has not lost any of its original impact and his criticisms of performance appraisal schemes of his time may seem equally relevant to current industrial practices. There is something naturally appealing in the proposition that if you ask someone to set his (or her) own goals, he will be more committed to achieving them than when targets are imposed upon him. Few will deny that consultation and participation provide a better basis for planning and control than autocratic management. But the managerial process – and that includes management appraisal – cannot ignore the needs of the organization, including the need for description and evaluation of various jobs in the managerial hierarchy, the need to identify what personal and technical skills are required for these jobs, the need for manpower planning, and finally the need to tell individuals how they perform and how they can improve their prospects for promotion and advancement.

A scheme for performance appraisal

All these require the organization to implement a scheme for performance appraisal as part of the overall managerial planning and control framework. McGregor is right in his observation that managers are reluctant to carry out appraisals, for all the reasons he mentions, and that consequently the appraisals are poor and unreliable. He is also right to encourage self-appraisals, which should help employees to become better aware of the demands of the organization and more self-critical, and thereby perhaps become more realistic in their expectations. But the suggestion that self-appraisal, albeit with the aid and guidance of the employee's superior, is sufficient for management control purposes, is a delusion. The responsibility for appraising the performance of subordinates must lie with their managers.

What should an appraisal scheme consist of? Appraisal is not an exact science and views as to what it should cover are bound to vary. There are many organizations in which the appraisal is confined to personal traits, such as intelligence, judgement, initiative, integrity, ability to withstand stress, and so on. The assessor is

156

required to grade each trait, or to tick one of several rubrics, so that a profile of personal traits is then revealed. The problem with such a scheme is that it is entirely divorced from the particular job of the appraised manager. He (or she) may be a paragon of virtue, but ill suited to his job, since some personal traits are more relevant to the execution of certain tasks than others. At the same time, it may be similarly argued that a scheme that completely ignores personal traits and is only concerned with job execution, is also deficient. It, too, can only provide a partial picture, from which it would be difficult to deduce whether a particular manager could perform well in another job, involving a different set of tasks and responsibilities.

There is clearly a need for a wider appraisal framework, such as the one suggested in the diagram in Figure 14.1. It is stipulated that there are basically four areas that a comprehensive appraisal scheme should cover, shown under two major headings.

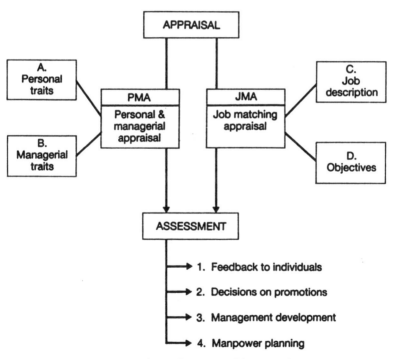

Figure 14.1 The appraisal framework

157

PMA – personal and managerial appraisal

A PERSONAL TRAITS

As mentioned above, these are relatively independent of the job situation, though it is quite conceivable that the perception of personal traits could be greatly influenced by the way a manager responds to the challenges of his (or her) job. For example, his judgement, or initiative, even intelligence, may receive different scores in two different job situations, not just because of differences between assessors, but because his responses to problems and stimuli may be (or may just seem to be) more intelligent, or exhibit better judgement, in one job as opposed to another. Similar remarks can be made about the other areas, and it is evident, therefore, that each of the four areas listed here cannot be viewed in isolation, since they are all interlinked in one way or another.

B MANAGERIAL TRAITS

These may be regarded as an extension of personal traits, and the appraisal would aim at making a judgement about the manager's ability to manage people and to interact with them. The traits normally considered in this way would include communication skills, cooperation, relationships with subordinates and superiors, loyalty, ability to generate enthusiasm and a sense of purpose, and above all that elusive quality of leadership – charisma.

JMA – job matching appraisal

C JOB REQUIREMENTS

Here the appraisal would attempt to determine the degree to which the manager meets the specifications laid down in his (or her) job description. This description usually starts off by defining the purpose of the job and proceeds to list the duties and responsibilities involved. It specifies the skills and qualifications required for the job, and the kind of experience that the job holder should have gained previously. It then usually indicates the range of activities and responses expected of the job holder in a variety of circumstances, both in routine tasks and in those that are ad hoc in nature. In particular, the appraisal would aim to ascertain how the manager responds to changing conditions, including the degree to which he is merely reactive, as opposed to being pro-active.

D ACHIEVING OBJECTIVES

In addition to the job description, the organization has specific expectations which are related to the corporate plan. The overall objectives of the enterprise need to be translated to a set of objectives for every department and every manager in terms of specific performance criteria appropriate for that job, such as profit and sales targets, costs and budget ceilings, improvements in quality and utilization of facilities. This process is often referred to as MBO (management by objectives). While the job description may often remain unchanged from year to year, or from quarter to quarter, the individual objectives set for the job holder may well be updated and modified from time to time, in accordance with the requirements of the corporate plan. The appraisal would aim to establish how the manager has coped with his objectives and whether he has met, or even managed to improve upon, the set targets.

Assessment leading to action

Thus, the four areas constitute distinct models of expectations. The first two cover personal and mangerial traits respectively and are aimed at the assesssment of a person as an individual and as a manager, but not in his capacity as a specific job holder. This is shown in the diagram in the box marked 'personal and managerial appraisal' (PMA). The other two areas are oriented towards the job requirements, covering its specifications and objectives, which feed into the box marked 'job matching appraisals' (JMA), the aim of which is to determine whether the job holder manages to do what is expected of him.

The results of PMA and JMA then form the basis for an overall assessment and action, as shown at the bottom of the diagram:

1 FEEDBACK

The appraised manager needs to know how his performance is judged by the organization, whether there are any areas where he needs to improve, and what his prospects are for further development and career progression. In some organizations this feedback is a formal affair, the results of the appraisal being read aloud to the manager and discussed with him in some detail, and he is even encouraged to record his own comments, so that his response to the appraisal is then on file for future reference.

2 STAFF PROMOTIONS

The personnel department is obviously concerned with such questions as: is the manager ready for promotion, immediately or at some future date? What should his next job be? What is his overall potential and what job would be appropriate for him in ten years' time? Allied to these questions are those associated with remuneration in terms of basic pay, bonuses, merit awards, and other benefits.

3 MANAGEMENT DEVELOPMENT

One of the important objectives of the appraisal system is to reveal areas in which an individual could benefit from further training in order to improve his current performance, or as part of the process of being groomed for his next job. Management development is an investment in the future. It can be expensive and it is generally time-consuming. Managers often begrudge the time spent away from the job on some courses, which do not promise immediate tangible benefits, and this is why a formal procedure is required to identify management development needs and to ensure that those requiring training over a specified planning horizon get the opportunity to learn and improve.

4 MANPOWER PLANNING

Finally, the results of the appraisal process are invaluable for manpower planning purposes. In order to ensure that the enterprise continues to operate smoothly in the future, and that suitable managers are available to cater for whatever expansion programmes and other changes are envisaged, the organization needs to have an adequate stock of people of the right calibre and potential to fill the crucial future managerial slots in the hierarchy. I recently visited an organization in which it transpired that all the top ten executives were scheduled to retire within a period of two years; in another organization it was discovered that there was a serious shortage of first-class people at certain middle management grades, so that an ambitious expansion programme that had been planned for a long while could well be in jeopardy. These are just two examples where well-conducted management appraisals could have provided essential information to the manpower planning process.

Conclusion

As indicated above, most managers concede that, in principle, management appraisal is necessary, and many organizations operate appraisal exercises of sorts, though only a few operate comprehensive systems that encompass all the ingredients indicated in the diagram. Those that do, tend to become rather bureacratic, the appraisers tend to be cautious, and the results tend to converge and become undiscriminating. As a consequence, there is a danger that the systems will fall into disrepute and be regarded as a waste of time. If assessing students in a class culminates with an 'A' grade for all of them, it is questionable whether the grading system has any value.

This danger has to be faced, by constantly reminding assessors of the purpose of the excerise, by making them aware of the need to take it seriously, by training them to become better and more reliable assessors, and by refining and modifying the system in the light of experience. It is certainly a grave mistake to delegate this responsibility permanently to outside professional agencies. Assessing managers is too important to be ignored or neglected, and it is too important to be left to the professionals.

References

Drucker, P. 1954. *The Practice of Management*. New York: Harper and Row.

Eilon, S. 1979. *Aspects of Management* (2nd edn). Oxford: Pergamon Press.

Maslow, A. H. 1954. *Motivation and Personality*. New York: Harper and Row.

McGregor, D. 1957. An uneasy look at performance appraisal. *Harvard Business Review*, 35, 89–94. Also published in his collection of essays *Leadership and Motivation* (chapter 12). Cambridge, Mass.: MIT Press, 1966.

Taylor, F. W. 1911 (reprinted 1947). *Scientific Management* (incorporating: Shop management, The principles of scientific management and Testimony before the Special House Committee). New York: Harper and Row.

CHAPTER 15

What makes Sammy run?

Organizational goals and structure

In Chapter 13 we discussed one of the basic tenets of the managerial process – accountability – and in Chapter 14 we dwelt on the logical consequence of accountability, namely on the question of appraisal of managerial performance. The rationale for accountability emanates from the concept of hierarchical goals. For the management of an enterprise to be able to plan its future activities and control its operations, it must first determine the direction in which it wishes to proceed (i.e. the overall policy) and then specify the corporate goals or objectives in the form of quantifiable desiderata, which can serve as bench-marks against which the performance of the enterprise can subsequently be judged. These corporate goals then need to be translated into a series of divisional and departmental goals within the organizational structure, so that every part of the enterprise fully understands what needs to be accomplished, with reference to a specified timetable, in order to ensure that the overall corporate goals are attained.

This hierarchical formulation of goals, starting at the top and working through to the operating level, is the essence of the organizational structure and the basis on which responsibility and accountability of departments, groups and individuals is ultimately defined. The goal framework is shown by the first block in the diagram in Figure 15.1, with the arrows indicating the sequence of objective setting and organizational demarcation throughout the structure. The hierarchical goals then lead to determining the conditions under which the operations need to be performed, and this is shown by the operational framework in the second block in the diagram.

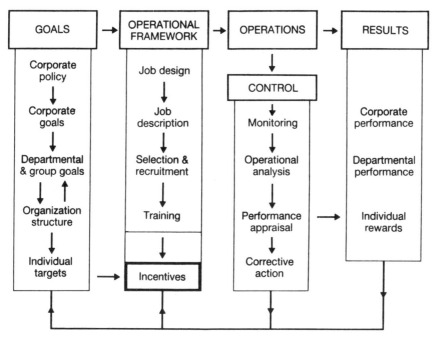

Figure 15.1 The place of incentives in the managerial process

It may be argued that determining the organization structure, shown in the first block, should in fact be incorporated as part of the second block, since the structure is an integral part of the operational framework. Its inclusion in the first block is merely a convenient way of drawing attention to the fact that departmental goals and organization structure are closely interlinked (as shown by the arrows pointing in both directions) and that clarity about the structure is a prerequisite to any system that assigns individual targets.

The operational framework

It has often been remarked that an effective industrial organization is like a symphony orchestra, where every player has a clearly designated and specific score, and where the coordinated performances of all the individual players combine to produce the beautiful

163

music envisaged by the composer. The key to success is that each player knows exactly what to play and when to play, and the analogy in the industrial scene is obvious enough. This is why well-managed organizations, and particularly those which involve a large number of stable and routine tasks, devote a great deal of effort to job design and job descriptions, aiming to eliminate – as far as possible – the incidence of uncertainty and ambiguity, in relation both to job content and to demarcation of responsibility.

But formulating a hierarchy of goals and producing well-thought-out organization charts are not enough. Not only is there a need for everyone in the organization to know precisely what his (or her) job is, to appreciate how it affects the work of others and to understand how it fits into the wider corporate context, every individual must also have the necessary aptitude and skill to perform the job effectively and efficiently.

This is where personnel selection, recruitment, training and performance appraisal play such a crucial part in the managerial planning and control process. In too many organizations, in the UK and elsewhere, management is content to assign tasks and performance targets without ensuring that operators and managers are both suitable and capable of doing their jobs. And even where these issues are handled with care when individuals are first assigned their tasks and responsibilities, there is a need for a periodic audit to detect whether any deterioration has set in and to determine how improvements can be implemented.

The arrows in the diagram generally refer to the sequence in which activities need to be implemented, but in reality they are all subject to an elaborate iterative process. For example, the second block depicts the need for job design, followed by job description, followed by recruitment, followed by training. In fact, job design may well be affected by job description, by the qualities and capabilities of the recruited personnel and by feedback from the training programme. Similarly, in the third block, monitoring the operations, studying their effectiveness (operational analysis), and appraising the performance of employees are all interlinked, and the process of measurement and monitoring, for example, may have to be modified to take account of the findings of operational analysis and performance appraisals. Not all these feedback links are shown in the diagram, which otherwise would have become too cluttered to present a coherent picture, and only the main links between the blocks are therefore depicted.

Incentive schemes

It has long been argued, by academics and practitioners alike, that the systematic planning and control function, described in Figure 15.1, would be incomplete without the design of incentives. It is equally clear, though, that an incentive scheme on its own, without the rest of the paraphernalia in the diagram, could be aimless and arbitrary, even harmful. The purpose of incentives is to influence employee attitudes and behaviour in ways that give the employees satisfaction and at the same time enhance the overall goals of the organization.

There is a bewildering variety of carrot and stick incentives that can be designed, as suggested by the list in Table 15.1. This is not a comprehensive list, but it includes the most common forms of inducement found in industry. Broadly, they fall into five categories: immediate cash rewards, monetary-equivalent rewards, deferred rewards, non-monetary incentives and negative incentives.

The first category of monetary rewards consists of three groups: a fixed remuneration package that does not depend on performance, neither individual nor corporate, and usually consists of salary and fixed bonuses (in some countries a 'thirteenth month' salary is provided to eligible employees at the end of the financial or calendar year, mainly to induce them to stay in the company); the second group is usually added to the fixed remuneration and is related to the performance of the individual or his (or her) employee group; the third is related to corporate performance.

The second category shown in the table consists of a wide range of monetary-equivalent rewards, namely benefits and gifts that have a distinct monetary value for the recipient. The third category concentrates on deferred rewards ('jam tomorrow'), the fourth category consists of non-monetary inducements and the fifth in-cludes disciplinary measures for non-performers. Details of these five categories are listed in the table and are further discussed below. Needless to say, the overall package for an individual employee may be a composite of several ingredients.

Table 15.1 Five types of incentives

1 *Monetary rewards*

    (a) Not performance related
- salary
- Christmas/year-end fixed bonus
- 'thirteenth month' salary

    (b) Individual/group performance related
- reward proportional to individual output
- reward proportional to group output
- commission (e.g. on sales)
- merit award for excellence

    (c) Corporate performance related
- annual bonus
- profit sharing

2 *Monetary-equivalent rewards*
- car, telephone
- medical insurance for self and family
- life, accident and disability insurance
- paid tuition fees for employees' children
- holidays, paid spouse travel
- paid club subscriptions, entertainment allowance
- discount on the company's products or services
- discount on travel and purchases from selected outlets
- low-interest loans and house mortgage
- interest-free loan to purchase the company's shares
- prizes, gifts and gift vouchers, long-service awards
- other benefits in kind (e.g. accommodation, clothing)

3 *Deferred rewards ('jam tomorrow')*
- promotion and promotion prospects
- pension schemes
- stock options
- deferred bonuses

4 *Non-monetary rewards*
- status, job title
- peer recognition, sense of ownership
- plaques, certificates, 'mention in dispatches'
- promotion
- spacious office, carpet, expensive office furniture

5 *Negative incentives ('the stick')*
- reprimand, caution, negative points system
- loss of pay, loss of perks and privileges
- sideways move, demotion
- dismissal

Ten rules for incentive schemes

Personnel managers generally advocate that the design and maintenance of incentive schemes should follow ten golden rules:

1   Pay incentives are important, but incentives are not confined to monetary rewards.
2   Desirable attainment levels should be clearly specified, for which corresponding individual rewards would ensue.
3   A clear connection needs to be established between attainment and individual effort and responsibility.
4   Individual attainments need to be compatible with departmental and organizational goals.
5   Individual attainment should not conflict with the scope of attainment by others.
6   Facilitating others to achieve their goals should also be rewarded.
7   The scope for gaining rewards should not be jeopardized by structural changes in the organization or reporting relationships.
8   The ability to secure achievable reward levels should not be adversely affected by changes to the incentive scheme which are specifically aimed at restricting in the future what the employee has already managed to achieve in the past.
9   A positive incentive scheme can be effectively enhanced by a system of penalties for undesirable results or modes of behaviour.
10 Every scheme needs to be periodically reviewed to ensure that its major objectives, as part of the integrated system described in the diagram, remain valid.

The rationale for these so-called golden rules may seem self-evident at first, but some of the statements are rather simplistic and their rigid application in practice may well lead to unfortunate consequences, as the following comments would suggest.

Rule 1: Non-monetary rewards

Monetary incentives are the most talked about, but the existence of elaborate schemes for non-monetary rewards in many companies suggests that they too are very popular with employers and employees. Some of these rewards have a monetary equivalent, such as paid holidays, extra 'business travel' and paid spouse travel, entertainment allowance, paid club memberships, paid children's tuition fees and scholarships, assorted gifts and gift vouchers (sometimes related to a positive points-scoring system), better company car, accommodation, clothing, and a variety of other perks.

It is often pointed out that all these extras are equivalent to raising the employee's basic salary and that if he (or she) had a higher disposable income he would have a choice of purchasing what he needs or wants, rather than be encumbered with unwanted gifts. In addition, the income tax authorities have been paying increasing attention to what they call 'benefits in kind', and taxing them as money equivalents has made them less attractive than they used to be. However, it would seem that more often than not such awards are generally welcomed by the employee and his family and that the publicity given to award winners within the organization and the local community has an added important social dimension, which the recipients greatly appreciate. The further advantage to the company is that some non-monetary rewards are usually one-off and are, therefore, more flexible and less costly than permanent salary increases.

As shown in Table 15.1, a special category of money-equivalent awards is that of the 'jam tomorrow' kind, of which stock options and non-contributory pension schemes are the most prominent. The prospect of capital appreciation and the provision of security for old age have proved enticing to many employees. Some of the schemes, particularly those involving stock options, are so designed as to yield benefits only at some future date, provided the individual remains employed by the company.

Some merchant and investment banks have found that such schemes serve as effective golden handcuffs that prevent selected key employees from leaving. Deferred bonuses for past performance, which accumulate for several years and are payable only to those in the company's employ on a predetermined future date, are designed to serve the same purpose. As the performance of these banks is primarily dictated by the quality of their staff, shackling some of them to the organization by the promise of future rewards becomes a very important feature in their strategy.

Genuine non-monetary rewards – namely those that do not have a direct cash equivalent for the employee – emphasize status and public recognition, and might include the award of a plaque for special achievement, which the recipient can proudly hang on the wall, 'mention in dispatches' at various meetings and in the company newspaper, invitations to meet important customers or foreign visitors, and so on (see Table 15.1).

In some American companies the office walls of middle managers are festooned with dozens of plaques, certificates and photographs signed by the 'great and the good'. In one company I came across a novel idea for public recognition, where the winner of the weekly competition for excellence, dubbed 'employee of the week', was given a parking space in the directors parking area in front of the head-office building for all the employees to note and applaud. Similar awards were given for the 'employee of the month' and 'employee of the year', and the directors made it their business to stop by for a photo-call and congratulate the winners on their achievements. Incidentally, it is interesting to note that if such a system were to be tried in Britain, it would probably prove to be a total failure, which suggests that the success and effectiveness of all incentive schemes, and particularly those of the non-monetary type, are culture-dependent.

Perhaps less ostentatious, but of potentially greater long-term value, is the award of extra training opportunities to widen the employee's range of skills and to improve his career prospects. The ultimate reward for excellence is, of course, promotion, which combines monetary and non-monetary rewards and is perhaps the most desired form of recognition by all ambitious employees. One often encounters cases where employees are happy to get promoted without immediate improvement in their remuneration package, confident that their enhanced status would not only result in financial rewards in due course, but give them greater authority over budgets and subordinates. For some, particularly at the higher echelons of the organization, the acquisition of power and responsibility is far more important than sheer cash.

However, many excellent employees are not necessarily suitable to undertake greater managerial responsibilities. Companies which nonetheless persist in promoting such individuals, until they truly reach their level of incompetence (the so-called 'Peter's principle'), soon experience an overall decline in efficiency and morale. There is a need, therefore, for good experienced staff, who cannot be promoted, to retain job satisfaction and gain recognition among their peers, by virtue of their special knowledge or status, by the fact that their advice is occasionally sought by senior managers, and even by the award of extra financial compensation in excess of that normally associated with their grade.

For some, the ability to participate in the planning and decision process is a means of encouraging a sense of belonging and ownership (the example of designating all the employees as 'partners' at the John Lewis department stores in Britain is well documented). For others the outward trappings of status are all-important, such as a spacious office, a nice carpet, or expensive office furniture, all of which help to enhance their recognition among their peers.

Rule 2: Attainments leading to rewards

The need to specify what attainment levels would merit an award stems from the argument that in the absence of such stipulation, there would be uncertainty as to what award (if any) should be given. It is suggested that employees may have no motivation to strive towards an unspecified objective, and that many would resent the fact that the rules for award are effectively determined 'after the event', so to speak, with management arbitrarily moving the goal posts.

This argument is certainly apposite at the operating level, where employees perform routine tasks and where responsibility to individuals can be easily assigned, for example on production lines, in maintenance work, and in repetitive clerical operations. But there are many instances where people work in teams, where individual contributions can only become effective as they merge into a team effort. Similarly, in many supervisory and managerial functions, particularly when the detailed ingredients of the job are difficult to define, or where discretion and proficiency are import-ant characteristics, specifying performance in quantitative terms may be either meaningless or misleading. In such cases, the overall performance of an individual is a matter for subjective judgement, so that rule 2 can hardly apply.

Rule 3: Individual contributions

Rule 3 seeks to specify a clear link between goal attainment and the individual's contribution and responsibility. When the validity of rule 2 is in doubt, some companies prefer to base the individual reward on a group or departmental incentive, given to all members of the group, in the form of a percentage on the individuals' basic salary. Others set aside a sum of money to be distributed to members of the department at the discretion of its manager, following individual performance appraisals.

Such a scheme allows flexibility both at the departmental level, in that different departments need not be awarded the same lump sum, and at the level of individual bonuses within any given department, so that differentials could reflect the perceived individual contribution made to the work of the department. Leaving the final allocation to the discretion of departmental managers reinforces their responsibility and accountability for the work of their teams.

Although rule 2 is ignored when group incentive schemes are put into practice, employees soon get used to the way these schemes operate and accept the discipline of peer pressure to perform well. Those who take objection to the subjective nature of the allocation process tend to vote with their feet and go elsewhere (assuming that alternative employment opportunities are available in the labour market and that employees have a genuine choice in the matter). The need to acquiesce with the objectives of the group, to be cooperative and to strive for collective success becomes overwhelming, though within the group there is competition between members for bigger slices of an allocated cake.

This system functions well in organizations where team work and team spirit are important, but it should be realized that by encouraging conformity and group allegiance, individual talent and flair may be dampened. Individualists simply do not perform to their full potential as anonymous members of groups. Organizations where individual flair is important, such as in R&D departments or innovative teams in merchant banks, have to create the conditions that allow such individuals to thrive, although their resultant prima donna status is often a cause for constant rivalry and friction.

Incidentally, where varying individual bonuses are employed, it is rare for details of the final bonuses to be formally publicized, since people are far more sensitive to differentials than to the absolute outcomes. This is not to say that some individuals do not share information about their pay and bonuses, and one often finds that news travels faster by word of mouth than by being pinned on the noticeboard, but individual disappointment is easier to bear when it is not publicly proclaimed.

Rule 4: Compatibility with organizational goals

The importance of rule 4, which seeks to harmonize the goals throughout the organization, can hardly be overemphasized. Ostensibly, the disaggregation of corporate goals into departmental and individual goals should ensure that the latter are compatible with the former (as suggested in Figure 15.1). In reality, though, individual goals tend to develop a life of their own and become increasingly divorced from the needs of the rest of the organization. Danger lurks here. In this context, the following common examples should be informative:

(a)   A purchasing clerk's pay is linked to his productivity, defined as the number of requisitions processed per month. It is therefore in his interest to break down orders sent to single suppliers and generate as many requisitions as possible. His pay increases as a result, but so does the amount of paperwork and the cost of processing. If, in addition, the company is offered an escalating discount, which depends on the value of each requisition, substantial savings to the company may be lost by the clerk's behaviour. Clearly his incentive scheme is not in alignment with the needs of the organization.

(b)   A distributor of domestic appliances has a group of repairmen to carry out service calls to customers. A repairman has an incentive scheme that links his pay to the number of calls made. The company, however, gets paid by the customers only for completed repairs. If a repair is not completed, because of

172

lack of a part, the repairman collects the part from the store the next morning and calls on the customer again. Here it is in the interest of the repairman not to complete the repair during the first call but to maximize the number of calls made. The result is an increase of pay for him, a horrendous increase in costs for the company, and a high number of customers dissatisfied with the level of service they get.

(c) The manager of a fleet of vehicles is responsible for their maintenance and is paid in proportion to the time that they are 'on the road'. The purpose of the incentive is to reduce down-time and the cost of hiring extra vehicles. To ensure that he does not run out of spare parts that are ever likely to be needed, the manager proceeds to build a very high stockpile of parts to cater for even the remotest eventuality. The result is that his pay increases, but the company is faced with high carrying costs for the stock of spare parts held.

(d) A salesman is paid commission on the value of goods sold to customers. He therefore proceeds to sell the 'easy' items in the catalogue and not necessarily those that yield the highest profit margin. In fact, he may be able to increase his commission substantially by selling items which the company regards as loss leaders. The more he sells (which is what the incentive encourages him to do), the less profitable the company becomes.

(e) A bank branch manager is encouraged to lend money to customers and is paid a commission in proportion to the total amount of money lent per annum. Although the manager is too conscientious to engage in reckless lending, he clearly has an incentive to lend even in marginal cases and thereby increase the probability of bad debts to the bank.

(f) A salesman of office equipment is allocated a quarterly target, which he must try to achieve. If the target is attained, he gets a bonus. At the same time, he is given discretion to offer discounts to 'suitable' customers. As a result, he tends to use his discretion extensively before the end of the quarter, so as not to lose his bonus. Customers who would otherwise have delayed their orders by a week or two are encouraged to place orders before the deadline, in order to benefit from the discount, but the resultant total sales revenue is lower than

173

it would have been, if the salesman had not been encouraged to be over-generous shortly before the end of the quarter. Similarly, when the salesman has already achieved his target and is already assured of his bonus, he begins to think of the next quarter and is inclined to defer taking further orders, so that sales income gets delayed and some orders may be lost (when no discount is forthcoming). In both cases, what is good for the salesman is not so good for the company.

In all these examples the design of the incentive scheme is incompatible with the goals of the organization, and in each case it is possible, and imperative, to amend the scheme to eliminate the conflict of interests. And yet, scheme designers are prone to adopt simplistic assumptions and often fail to appreciate the long-term consequences of their schemes, with the result that such examples are commonly found in many companies.

Rule 5: Conflict between individual aspirations

The goal disaggregation process may not only produce the type of mismatch just mentioned, between the goals of an individual and those of the organization, but often results in a mismatch between the goals of different individuals. This is what rule 5 aims to avoid, but while the former type of mismatch is avoidable, this cannot always be said about the latter. Even departmental goals are often in direct conflict with each other. Here are some common examples:

(a) The sales department in an organization is typically assigned the objective of maximizing sales revenue, while the production department is charged with the responsibility for minimizing costs. The former objective is enhanced by having as wide a product range as possible, the latter by curtailing product variety as far as possible (the ideal situation from the production manager's point of view is to produce only one product, thereby simplifying scheduling problems, reducing set-up times and saving on inventories). This is often cited as the classic inter-departmental conflict.

(b) Customer service seeks to ensure that product design should incorporate easy access for maintenance purposes and for replacement of parts while the manufacturing people champion the motto 'design for production', to help in the constant drive to reduce unit costs. The two aims reflect different design strategies and are not always compatible.

(c) In many companies quantity and quality are in conflict. When the pay of production employees is linked to output, they may be tempted to consider quality as a secondary issue, and this contrasts, of course with the objectives of those who have to sell the product and deal with customer complaints. This conflict is particularly evident in companies employing the piece-rate system at the shopfloor level. The financial incentive drives the employees to be solely concerned with output and to disregard the needs and aspirations of employees in other departments.

Rule 6: Rewards for facilitators

This rule aims to resolve the problem of how to provide incentives for those not directly assigned the responsibility for output-related operations. There are many employees, particularly in service functions, for whom individual output targets are quite inappropriate. Administrators, head-office managers, operational research analysts, R&D scientists and engineers, designers, product testers, market research specialists, staff in the finance and personnel departements, clerical staff, telephone operators, production planners and schedulers, maintenance personnel, cleaners, and indeed many others – they all perform important functions that enhance the wellbeing of the organization and contribute, directly or indirectly, to the efficiency of those who benefit directly from a performance-related incentive scheme.

The precise contribution of every member of the vast supporting cast is often extremely difficult to ascertain, and yet their collective role is vital, and the absence of due recognition and participation in bonuses and extra pay may well lead to justifiable resentment and frustration. Some companies operate a form of bonus for indirect workers, linked to the average bonus gained by direct workers or to corporate performance. In addition, the use of individual merit awards, determined by subjective managerial judgement, is often thought to be appropriate for supporting services.

Rule 7: Effects of organizational changes

Rule 7 seeks to reassure the employee that the incentive scheme would not be affected by factors outside his (her) control. As stated earlier, the purpose of the managerial process described in Figure 15.1 is to produce a consistent and stable framework for determining individual responsibility and accountability, and for assigning individual tasks and rewards.

However, the industrial scene is constantly changing. The company expands or contracts, product design and the product range are periodically modified, technical specifications and quality requirements change, new manufacturing methods replace old ones, and the same applies to marketing and distribution methods. All these changes, stimulated by technological advance, by competition and by the economic environment, are bound to affect the organizational structure and individual job descriptions. The methodology described in Figure 15.1 is not a once-and-for-all exercise, but a continuous process. It therefore follows that an incentive scheme enjoyed by an employee, or a group of employees, may become inappropriate or obsolete when circumstances change.

Rule 7 suggests that, whatever potential an individual employee has for earning under a given incentive scheme, this should not be diminished when the scheme is overhauled or scrapped. Clearly, no company could subscribe to such an idea for long, and as a general principle rule 7 must be considered as impractical.

Rule 8: Changes in products and working practices

There are many cases, however, where conflict arises elsewhere. The general environment may not change and the organization may continue to support the basic structure of the pay incentive scheme, but managers argue that, due to some changes in design specifications of the product or changes in the manufacturing processes, the bonus rates related to performance should be subject to change.

Take the example of an operator capable on a good day of producing 1000 pieces, but with a new and faster machine, he may be able to produce 1500, without any extra effort. If the pay is output-related, he would ostensibly be entitled to a 50% increase in take-home pay, and yet in this case the increased production rate is entirely due to the capital expenditure in the new machine. The operator would naturally resent a cut in the bonus rate, but the strict application of rule 8 is quite untenable.

Admittedly, unscrupulous employers have been known to exploit even marginal or cosmetic changes in the working environment as excuses to review their incentive schemes and restrict what they perceive as excessive pay. Three interesting examples may be cited in this context to illustrate the consequences of rule 8, although these examples are equally applicable to our earlier discussion of rule 4:

(a) In manufacturing industry, flat piece rates are often based on what a rate fixer (or a work study engineer) expects an average operator to achieve on a normal working day. But skill, speed and the effect of the learning curve vary widely among operators, and some may easily achieve two or three times the envisaged average output. There have been many cases where management felt that the results achieved by the best operators were too high, causing embarrassingly large differentials in take-home pay compared with other employees. Accordingly, they sought to amend the flat piece rate in a way that reduced the marginal rate gained for high levels of output. Operators have typically responded by restricting their official output and have resorted to 'banking', that is, concealing physical output above a certain level to be 'declared' at some convenient future date.

(b) Fierce competition between computer manufacturers has prompted one company to introduce a generous commission scheme for the sales force. To sharpen the competition between the salesmen, their quarterly commissions were widely publicized in the company newspaper. Revenue rose sharply, but one salesman was exceptionally successful and his take-home pay exceeded that of the chief executive by a very wide margin. The chief executive said he did not mind, but his fellow directors did, and so did many managers in the production and support functions, whose contributions to the wellbeing of the company seemed dwarfed by the special treatment meted out to the successful sales boys. Resentment grew and eventually the chief executive had to put a ceiling on the level of commission earned.

(c)   A similar experience is often encountered in merchant and investment banks, where high rewards (whether they are in the form of commissions or of bonuses) are the order of the day. Annual individual bonuses for performance are often determined on the basis of a subjective judgement exercised by special panels (which, in each case, includes the individual's boss). The subjective nature of the appraisal, and the fact that the outcome is greatly influenced by the opinion of the individual's boss, are bound to lead to adverse reactions at times, but for most of the staff the system works reasonably well. Its main merit is that it allows a great deal of flexibility, since the amounts allocated vary widely from year to year, thereby putting everyone on his (her) toes. The distribution of individual bonuses in any one year is also very wide – in one American investment bank some senior executives have been known to gain 400% or more of basic salary. However, the detailed figures are not publicized and the bank decided as a matter of policy that, in order to encourage staff to continue to do their best, no ceiling on earnings should be promulgated. Experience suggests that rule 8 can be maintained in merchant and investment banks, but in other industries, as indicated by some of the previous examples, such a system would eventually prove to be unworkable.

Rule 9: Rewards and penalties

The list of incentives in Table 15.1 is a mixture of carrots and sticks. While the first four categories are carrots of various kinds, rule 9 draws attention to the need for negative incentives as well, such as those shown in the fifth category.

The organization is anxious to ensure that employees follow all the laid-down procedures, in relation to their work, in relation to each other, and in relation to customers. Where customer service is of prime importance, the device of the 'mystery shopper' is often used, whereby a member of the inspection department, or an employee of an external agency, pretends to be a customer and reports on the quality of service that he (she) experienced. The fear of being reprimanded, of having to forgo financial rewards, of missing promotion prospects, and ultimately even losing one's job, is part of the discipline that the organization wishes to impose in order to ensure adherence to the instructions given. However, if the instructions are too rigidly applied, and if the fear of retribution becomes very worrying for employees, there is a danger of stifling initiative and encouraging an attitude of risk aversion. Here are two examples:

(a) We referred earlier to the case of the bank branch manager who is urged to lend money to customers. In one bank, bad debt is strongly disapproved of, leading to severe reprimands and block of promotion for those responsible. As a result, the manager tends to become over-cautious and refuses lending applications whenever he has the slightest reason to suspect that the loan might turn sour. The loss of business to the bank, resulting from this excessive desire to avoid risk, is enormous.

(b) The R&D department is encouraged to develop new inventions and designs, but is warned that the penalty for product failure, once it is released to the market, would be instant dismissal. The R&D staff would naturally become very reluctant to sanction production before prototypes undergo extensive field tests, but excessive caution may well mean long delays and loss of market opportunities.

Rule 10: Need for periodic reviews

This rule states the obvious need to monitor, evaluate and revise the incentive scheme from time to time, to take account of changing circumstances and to reassess its perceived effectiveness. The very application of this rule implies that it is not compatible with the spirit of rules 7 and 8.

Apart from the fact that changing internal organizational and operational conditions must affect the revision of existing incentive schemes, there is a need to consider developments elsewhere in the industry and the general social and economic climate within which the schemes have to operate. For example, piece-rate systems used to be very popular in manufacturing industry for many years, but because of changing attitudes to the piece-rate philosophy, they have become far less prevalent. Instead, there has been an increasing emphasis in recent years on schemes which are not individually output-related, such as bonuses and corporate performance-related systems, coupled with deferred rewards and non-monetary incentives. All these developments underline the importance of rule 10.

Conclusion

There are three main lessons to be drawn from this discussion. The first is that incentive schemes are an integral part of the managerial planning and control process, as pointed out in Figure 15.1, and cannot therefore be considered in isolation. The second is that there is a bewildering variety of schemes that can be devised, as shown in Table 15.1, and the selection of the right combination calls for a great deal of foresight and ingenuity. Thirdly, golden rules can easily be formulated to guide personnel management in this area, but their apparent common sense may conceal contradictions and inconsistencies, and their rigid application may well lead to undesirable consequences. There is more to the simple carrot and stick philosophy than meets the eye.

CHAPTER 16

Don't spit in the soup, we all have to eat

How to reduce risk and uncertainty

'Right boys', said Prof. Roland Smith to his assistants. 'The foundation officials have queried a number of statements in our research proposal. They want further clarification of the objectives of the work, they want to know exactly how we are going to tackle the project, and they want to have a clear idea of what we plan to get out of it. So, let's get back to the word processor and produce a new proposal to meet their expectations.'

This scene is re-enacted over and over again in numerous universities and research establishments all over the world, and research workers in industry face similar problems, except that their research plans may not depend on an external grant-giving body and are usually judged internally. From time to time, every research group needs to produce some justification for its current budget, or for the allocation of future funds, and the decision makers in charge of the purse strings are constantly struggling to adjudicate between competing demands for scarce resources and are forced into making choices.

It is not surprising, therefore, that in order to assign priorities, they seek more and more information, with the expectation that comprehensive proposals, crammed with data and detailed schedules, would help to reduce uncertainties and increase the probability that the research would lead to tangible results. It would be refreshing to have a foundation that scorns all this paperwork and is content to allocate funds purely on the reputation and track record of the applicants, who – in the course of their research – would in fact be expected to depart from their declared initial programme and follow their intuition without inhibition. I have heard of one research-funding body in the medical field that does precisely that, but such an approach is regarded by many as too risky and is rather rare.

The rise of bureaucracy

The general desire to reduce uncertainty stems also from the need for decision makers to be accountable for their actions, and as they become more reluctant to make mistakes, the level of risk aversion throughout the process of managing R&D tends to increase. Furthermore, funding decisions are very often driven by committees – involving a peer review in the case of grant-giving bodies, such as charitable foundations, and appropriations committees in industry – and committees tend to be conservative, since they rely heavily on consensus and compromise. The greater the pressure on limited resources and the more accountable those participating in the decision process, the more bureaucratic the process becomes.

As bureaucracy increases, so does the level of frustration of research workers and innovators. I have often heard the exasperated comment from an applicant for funds that if he could specify in great detail what results would emerge from the proposed research project, there would be no need to ask for money to carry out the work. It has also been suggested that many applicants purport to forecast detailed results, which are none other than those already obtained in their most recent projects. In this way the risk of not achieving the objectives enumerated in the research proposal is eliminated and the allocated funds can be used to finance the next stage in the research programme. Such a system means that the allocated funds in fact represent a reward for *work already done*, as opposed to *proposed future work*. By appending published papers and detailed reports to a research proposal as 'proof of tangible results', the chances of getting approval seem to increase significantly, though the real efforts of the research programme may in fact be directed to producing a case for the next proposal.

Lateral consistency

This dilemma, between the need to explore and innovate on the one hand and the formalized and bureaucratic adjudication process on the other, is not confined to research and development, but poses a serious challenge to the prevalent managerial ethos of an organization. I referred to this problem some time ago in an article entitled 'Lateral consistency' (Eilon 1985), when I tried to contrast the basic need for an enterprise to function on the basis of consistency and order with the need to encourage creativity and embrace change. Clearly, it is essential for an organization to follow set procedures, to ensure that decisions are consistent with each other and that there is a rational framework within which all managerial actions can be accommodated. At the same time, the managerial hierarchy needs to ensure that the enterprise does not get staffed solely with organization yes-men, all anxious to toe the official line and please the boss. It is essential to have some mavericks with independent minds, who generate novel ideas, and who usually despise the rules.

Such original thinkers need to be positively encouraged, to stimulate unorthodox views and allow fresh challenges to be considered. In this way, a flow of innovations would constantly feed into a wide range of managerial functions, from product diversification and design, to marketing and production, even to employee recruitment and motivation.

The nurturing of creative thinking cannot, however, proceed at random; it too needs some logical framework within which it can be managed. And this is where the dilemma of 'lateral consistency' arises: 'the dilemma of how to achieve coexistence between consistency and innovation. No organization can survive for long on the one without the other. We need both: in fact we need a structured way in which the unstructured can be tolerated and brought to the fore' (Eilon 1985).

Corporate pathfinding leadership

Harold Leavitt picks up this topic in his book entitled *Corporate Pathfinders* (1986), in which he discusses the major problems

183

facing American management today. His thesis is that the management process consists of three parts – *pathfinding, problem solving*, and *implementing* – which he proceeds to define as follows (p. 3):

> Pathfinding is about getting the right questions rather than the right answers. It is about making problems rather than solving them. It is *not* about figuring out the best way to get there from here, nor even about making sure that we get there. It is rather about pointing to where we ought to go. Pathfinding ... is about mission, purpose and vision. Problem solving is about analysis, planning and reasoning; and implementing is about doing, changing, and influencing.

He further argues that problem solving has been the great preoccupation of business schools, with their emphasis on model building and a wide portfolio of analytical methods. 'That's the place to learn all about linear programming, systems analysis, operations research, and econometric methods, about how to build marketing models and how to do financial analyses.... Go to business school to learn to program what has previously been unprogrammable' (1986: 9). In this respect, he suggests, business schools are no different from other professions that rely heavily on analytical skills, such as engineering, accountancy and law. 'They require logic, consistency, and orderliness.'

In contrast, implementing requires working with and through people, by persuading them to cooperate and making *them* do the work (which is the essence of delegation). While implementation skills are not amenable to rigid formulation by mathematical equations, they are widely recognized in the business world as essential ingredients of the managerial process, and to a varying degree they too are included in MBA programmes, though for the most part these skills are acquired and perfected through experience.

What is inadequately represented in the American industrial culture, in Leavitt's view, and remains sadly undervalued, is pathfinding leadership, to provide a sense of vision, to transform business and to free it from the shackles of a highly structured bureaucracy. In an age of fast technical change, we need to ensure that new opportunities are not missed, particularly as far as new products and designs are concerned, though the same sentiment applies to innovation in marketing, production, organization structure and management control.

These problems are particularly acute for large corporations, where independent thinkers are often treated with suspicion and mistrust. Some are condemned to obscurity and end up as frustrated minor officials with little chance of making any impact on the complacent bureaucracy around them. Others have the courage to leave and start on their own. It is perhaps not surprising that many new ideas in the computer and information industry have blossomed in small companies, in spite of their relatively meagre financial and manpower resources, compared with some giant corporations that are household names.

Problem solvers and pathfinders

As an example to illustrate the divergent approaches of pathfinding, problem solving (or analysis), and implementation, Leavitt tells the story of a company employing some 5000 people with a turnover of $600 million a year, where the chairman posed the following question: Assuming that he had a free choice, and leaving aside any consideration of cost, what kind of corporation should he aim for? (1976: 49–54).

Leavitt describes how the implementer would approach this problem by seeking ways in which he could involve the workforce, and in his example this was epitomized by the vice-president for human resources wanting to run an opinion survey in order to elicit information from the employees. While Leavitt does not entirely dismiss this approach, since it may well generate some new ideas (like 'changing the colors of the office walls'), is it not – he asks – a case of the blind leading the blind, with a great deal of effort going into producing rather superficial and often trivial answers?

Leavitt then turns to the fundamental difference between the approaches of the problem solver and the pathfinder. He postulates that the problem solver – 'a true blue systems analyst, complete with MBA and computer terminal' – would say: 'Before deciding what the organization ought to look like in five years, we must first know as much as possible about what the relevant world will look like in five years.' This would lead to an elaborate exercise in forecasting the state of the economy, the market and the population, as well as the likely behaviour of the competitors. In short, the analyst's mode of thinking would be what Leavitt characterizes as 'orderly and logical', even though experience has taught us that most forecasts tend to be wrong, so that the very foundation on which the analyst would base his (or her) eventual conclusions might well turn out to be rather shaky.

In complete contrast, 'the pathfinding approach begins by asking us to look inward rather than outward, to think subjectively even as we confront objective reality', (and by asking) 'What do we really want to do with this company? What do we value? What kind of organization do we believe to be right and beautiful? What kind of organization would we love to build? In short, the pathfinder starts with a vision, with an idea of where he wants to be, not with where he is.

This is why, Leavitt concludes, problem solvers and pathfinders 'aren't usually on the same wavelength', they start from different premises, and they think differently, as suggested by the different names which he cites from the literature for the two approaches: *convergent versus divergent thinking, holistic versus particularistic, logical versus intuitive*. The two seem quite irreconcilable. And yet, as Leavitt puts it, 'if both imaginative and analytic styles are important to the management process (and this seems to be so) and if they have trouble living together, how can we get them to coexist harmoniously within the same person or the same organization?' (1986: 60).

Organizational implications

One organizational solution is to have two groups of people, one dominated by, or consisting solely of, analysts, and the other consisting of lateral thinkers. Both would ponder about the current and future states of the company, the first group within well-defined terms of reference and the second with a looser agenda. Both sets of solutions and ideas would be fed to the top, and if the senior executives are sufficiently broad-minded in their outlook and understanding of the processes involved, then the organization as a whole would benefit from this dual approach; it would be less prone to ignore novel ideas for launching new products and innovative trading and management methods, while continuing to operate within a logical structure and maintaining a consistent administrative framework that middle managers seem to be comfortable with. However, the problem of how to keep the peace between such divergent groups within the same organization remains, and only few companies, having tried this formula, can claim successful coexistence for long.

A more common approach is to buy intuitive, free-ranging and independent input from the outside. In the advertising field, for example, outside agencies are widely employed, very often at vast expense and in preference to internal departments. The rationale is that advertising is a highly imaginative (and well-paid) occupation, requiring artistic and creative minds, so that the successful individuals in that field are not likely to choose to become employees within a conservative environment of a stifling bureaucracy. Similarly, in the area of product development and design, many large companies are content to subcontract work to specialized small firms, though they often have well-endowed departments of their own working in this area.

The adoption of externally commissioned designs is quite common in the textile and fashion industry, for jewellery, furniture and many household goods, and even for cars and engineering products. As for managerial functions, it is not uncommon to have external advisers to contribute new ideas on production and marketing methds, personnel recruitment and assessment, as well as on organizational design, or to serve as confidants to the chief executive. Management consultants thrive on this kind of work. There is, therefore, an organizational solution to the problem of how to get the best of both worlds, without having to accommodate divergent groups under the same organizational umbrella: namely, to buy some original and imaginative thinking resources from the outside, although this may have serious implications for the scope, staffing and morale of the relevant internal groups.

Are lateral thinkers born or bred?

There are, however, two more fundamental questions that need to be asked. First, can skills embedded in pathfinding, imagination and lateral thinking be taught at all? Secondly, if they can, should training be directed only to individuals with the right aptitude, or is it possible to inculcate both qualities of analysis and lateral thinking in the same individuals?

The answer to the first question must be in the affirmative, if we believe that schools of art, design, architecture and literature, as well as a multitude of other courses in the arts, enhance a creative ability rather than stifle it. Admittedly, throughout history there have been outstanding artists and writers who had not had any formal training in their craft, and perhaps they would not have become so great if they had had it. But for the majority, it is generally agreed that formal education and training have been beneficial and stimulating.

The answer to the second question, of whether it is possible to combine two seemingly contradictory philosophies in the same training course, is less obvious. It has been suggested that the teaching methodology in many courses, for example in science and engineering, moulds students to develop and reinforce a vertical thinking discipline, causing their level of imagination to be progressively eroded during their course of studies and subsequent careers. In the same vein, serious criticisms have been voiced against business schools for producing hard-nosed and narrow-minded analysts, who are technique-bound and lack any imagination. Clearly, some of this criticism is justified. The structure of business schools, their traditions, their staff and the kind of problems that interest them and that they are able to teach – all these factors enhance the status quo and militate against change.

But change there must be. Business cannot subsist on analysis alone, nor can business schools. The changing economic climate, including the severe competition that now preoccupies the Western business world, means that – like industry – business schools need to adapt. They can no longer be content to train, in the terminology of Leavitt, only analysts and implementers. We need to develop teaching methodologies to encourage vision and imagination as well, and this difficult task must be the responsibility of business schools; there is simply no one else to do the job and, in any event, it would be a mistake to perpetuate the schism between the two cultures.

In the meantime, the critics should not rush in their zeal to write off the business schools. They would be wise to bear in mind the memorable phrase, attributed to the late President Johnson: 'Don't spit in the soup, we all have to eat.'

References

Eilon, S. 1985. *Management Assertions and Aversions*, Chapter 12. Oxford: Pergamon Press. Also in *Omega* 7 (3), 173–7.
Leavitt, H. J. 1986. *Corporate Pathfinders*. Homewood, Ill.: Dow Jones-Irwin.

CHAPTER 17

The role of business schools

Criticisms of business schools

As we have seen in earlier chapters, management theory and practice are in a state of flux. Although a great deal of empirical research has been carried out and hypotheses abound, there is, so far, no unified theory of management, while many recipes of 'how to do it' in practice lack any substantive foundation and more often than not turn out to be the hit-and-miss variety. And yet, there is a need for managers to learn from past experience and to appreciate what contributions various disciplines can make to the understanding and controlling of the business scene. It is generally expected that the appropriate place for this body of knowledge to be developed is in business and management schools.

A simple-minded concept of the role of these schools is to regard them as a link between would-be managers and industry. Young graduates want to pursue careers in business, while employers look for suitably qualified young people to fill vacancies in their organizations. The business schools may be said to complete the triangle, first by ascertaining what industry needs and then proceeding to convert the schools' intake into a product, which hopefully industry would be eager to buy. It is a simple and straightforward enough model – or is it?

In the previous chapter, reference was made to recent criticisms directed at business and management schools (the difference between the two types is minimal), not just with respect to some of the courses on offer, but directed at the whole approach and philosophy of management education. In the USA, where business schools have been operating for many decades, these criticisms are

190

said to come in cycles. There are times when the schools are held in very high esteem, with industry clamouring to recruit business graduates in droves, so much so that other university disciplines complain that, because of the great attraction of business careers, they fail to get a fair share of high-quality talent into their own graduate programmes. At other times, serious doubts are expressed about the ability of business schools even to comprehend the significance of the many changes that have taken place in the social and economic environment in recent years, let alone adjust to them. It is perhaps natural that these criticisms become particularly vocal when the economy is under pressure, and recent attacks on business schools may perhaps be attributed to the mounting frustration of American industrialists in having to cope with the challenge of overwhelming Japanese imports.

In the UK, management education has a much shorter pedigree (thirty years ago there were hardly any full-time management courses in British universities), so that industry is not populated with business graduates to anything like the extent that is prevalent in the USA. Critics, therefore, find it difficult to blame management education for the state of the UK economy, but this does not prevent them from expressing serious doubts about the value of this 'American import'.

The US and UK economies are often compared with certain prosperous countries which have not invested that heavily in university management education (such as Germany and Japan), the implication being that such investment is superfluous, or quite irrelevant, to the national economic wellbeing. Consequently, there are some British companies with international reputations and vast networks of subsidiaries abroad that, as a matter of policy, do not recruit business graduates at all, and there are many others that pay lip service to management education, but have a level of recruit-ment that constitutes only a small fraction of their managerial needs (this ambivalent attitude is shared by many industrial organizations in other countries in Western Europe).

What are the causes and rationale of these criticisms? They usually follow the publication of surveys of prospective employers and past graduates, aimed at determining their perceptions of what business schools do, and comparing expectations with reality. It is not intended to detail here the results of such surveys, but the

191

following brief comments may serve as a good indication of some of the key issues often raised.

Expectations of employers and business graduates

Employers usually expect business graduates to have a good knowledge (and not just scanty appreciation) of the social, economic and political environment in which the company operates, the special problems relating to its industrial sector, its range of products and markets, the nature of competition in general and in the industrial sector in particular, the legal requirements that govern all operations (including design, production, distribution, promotion, fair competition, and conditions of employment). They also expect business graduates to have a clear understanding of the way an enterprise operates, its organizational structure and the function of its constituent parts, the way various activities are planned and executed, the anticipation of outcomes, the essence of delegation, responsibility and accountability. Underlying all these requirements is the ability to analyse performance, to control and to communicate.

What employers often complain about is that business graduates are high on theory, but low in understanding on how it should be applied in practice, that they are technique-bound with little comprehension of real industrial problems, and that they lack the necessary personal skills to become effective managers. In addition, they are seen as a very expensive resource with inflated expectations of salary and career progression (this is a charge that is often expressed by British and Continental prospective employers, but is encountered in the United States as well).

As for the would-be graduates, their aims do not diverge markedly from those of the employers. They, too, want to become effective managers and are keen to acquire the knowledge and skills that would help them to that end. They expect that graduation from a business school would provide them with an admission ticket into the privileged managerial class, and the success of their predecessors serves to heighten expectations of rapid promotion and a prosperous future.

What they often complain about is that many of the detailed

techniques learnt on management courses are rarely applicable in practice, that the assumptions underlying the theories learnt in the classroom are remote from reality, and that the business environment encountered in their first job is quite different from the image gained during their studies. They also complain that it then takes too long to acclimatize, that industry (like the business school) does not encourage flair and imagination, and that consequently they are not given an opportunity fast enough to take responsibility and advance in the organizational hierarchy. It needs to be added here that in due course it is generally the conformists who rise to positions of responsibility and their innate conservatism perpetuates the status quo.

The response of the business school

The third partner in the triangle is the business school, which tries to look beyond the immediate recruitment needs of industry and to address itself to a more distant horizon. What the school needs to do, so the argument goes, is not to cater for management of today, but for management of tomorrow. This is why new techniques and concepts, which may be alien to practitioners today, need to be taught and inculcated into those who will assume responsible positions in the future. And this is why, coupled with the aspirations and promotion prospects of academic staff, business schools are keen on development of theory and on the advancement of academic disciplines.

The result is more analysis in depth of narrow problems, coupled with increasing complexity of model structures. Add to that the fact that many teachers in business schools have had little or no industrial experience (except, perhaps, shortly after graduation, when they were employed at a relatively junior level), and it becomes clear how the charge against the business schools' obsession with theory is thrown into sharp focus.

Attributes of management – the knowledge base

While not suggesting that the business schools are entirely blameless with respect to all these criticisms, the first question that needs to be asked is whether the expectations of both employers and graduates are really justified. Table 17.1 attempts to list the various ingredients that would be regarded as highly desirable for managers. They come under three headings: first, a knowledge base; secondly, personal skills; and thirdly, qualities of leadership and the 'art' of managing (some aspects of this issue are discussed in Chapter 5; see also Eilon (1979)).

The knowledge base consists of four elements, the first of which concerns the general environment. This element includes courses

Table 17.1 Management attributes – the needs

I The knowledge base

  1 The social–economic environment

    ● economics, social affairs, politics, the legal framework, etc.

  2 Industrial sectors

    ● engineering, shipping, banking, retailing and distribution, etc.

  3 The internal environment of the firm

    ● its ethos, organization, procedures

  4 Managerial functions

    ● personnel, production, finance, marketing, advertising, information technology, R&D, etc.

  5 Techniques

    ● modelling, measurement, monitoring and control, problem solving and analytical tools

II Personal skills

  Delegation
  Communication
  Presentation
  Persuasion
  Interviewing

III Qualities of leadership and the 'art' of managing

  Managing things
  Managing people
  Managing money
  Managing time
  Managing information
  Managing creativity
  Making decisions

in economics and the structure of industry, social science, industrial history, government policies that prescribe or affect the environment in which industry and business have to operate, the legal framework of business and its obligations to those affected by its activities (shareholders, customers, employees, suppliers and creditors). In addition, there are many other background subjects that are obviously appropriate for the understanding of the general socioeconomic system.

The more particular environment in which the firm has to operate is the industrial sector to which it belongs, such as engineering, mining, shipping, banking, distribution, and so on (this is the second element of the knowledge base, shown in Table 17.1). Government statistics list many industrial sectors, which differ greatly in their products and services, in their trading practices, and in the range of problems that face their management. In contrast to courses aimed at the general economic and social environment (referred to above), it is quite unrealistic to expect a business school to devote much time in its curriculum to a detailed study of the various industrial sectors. Constraints of time and available expertise, coupled with the fact that only very few students in any class would be interested in joining a particular sector (preferences in this respect often develop after students graduate, or only after experience of one or two jobs in industry), mean that any efforts in this direction have to be confined to specialized courses run specifically for the needs of each sector. Some business schools offer a certain amount of exposure to some business sectors, but such opportunities for specialization are inevitably limited and it is probable that the limited time available would be better devoted to more general subjects.

The specific internal environment concerns the organizational structure of the company, the demarcation of responsibilities and lines of communication between its entities, departmental aspirations and working practices, prevailing rules and procedures. All these may vary substantially from one organization to another and the best place to learn about them, and particularly to gain an understanding of the corporate ethos of an organization, is within the company itself through in-house training programmes, and not as part of an educational degree course at a business school.

The fourth element in the knowledge base in Table 17.1 concerns management functions, such as personnel, production, marketing and finance, etc. The prevailing argument is that these functions transcend the specific problems encountered in any particular industrial sector, so that knowledge gained in any given function in one sector is generally transferable to another. Most business schools attempt to provide sound training in managerial functions, though a comprehensive coverage is not feasible and students are often offered a choice of areas to specialize in.

The fifth element is concerned with techniques that transcend not only industrial sectors, but also managerial functions. Modelling techniques (such as resource allocation problems), measurement and monitoring processes, problem solving and analytical methods – these are general issues that face all industrial and business firms. This is why both the teaching of techniques, as well as of management functions, tends to become a predominant part of the business school curriculum. Together with the background subjects on the economic environment they constitute three of the four elements of the necessary knowledge base listed in Table 17.1, and these are widely acknowledged as most appropriate for inclusion in business curricula.

Further attributes – personal skills and leadership

The next set of attributes for effective management, shown in Table 17.1, is associated with personal skills. First and foremost, the manager must possess the ability to delegate work and responsibility to others. Then he (or she) needs to be able to communicate and discuss problems with colleagues, with subordinates and with superiors. Communication skills are not confined to proficiency in writing reports and handling paperwork, important as these undoubtedly are, but also to making oral presentations, explaining difficult and controversial issues, planning and steering group discussions, interviewing people for jobs, and eliciting information about facts and attitudes.

While latent skills of written and oral communications can be greatly enhanced by formal training, there are limits to the degree to which these topics can be accommodated in the time available in a school. There is also a general tendency in formal programmes to

give greater weight to written work, as opposed to oral presentation, though practices vary greatly from school to school.

The final set of desirable attributes in the table concerns qualities
of leadership and management skills, which – because of their
✕ somewhat nebulous and elusive character – are perhaps best
labelled 'the art of managing'. Management of resources encompasses many facets: managing things, managing people, managing
money, managing time and managing information – they all require
different skills and attitudes of mind, different blends of objective
analysis and warm compassion, different kinds of understanding of
the issues involved. There is also the intangible quality of management style and the ability to enthuse others with excitement and
esprit de corps. As for managing creativity, which is also listed in the
table, enough was said in the previous chapter to highlight the
many problems (as well as the benefits and risks) that have to be
faced.

But above all, an effective manager is exemplified by his ability to
make decisions, namely to scan the various alternatives offered to
him, to rise above short-term considerations and the immediate
pressures exerted on him, and to determine which path to follow.
This he is often expected to do with limited reliable information
and in the face of various risks and uncertainties. Perhaps this is the
attribute, in conjunction with the ability to inspire confidence
and motivate others, that is mostly associated with the quality of
leadership.

The making of managers

What scope is there for this range of decision-making attributes to
be formally taught at a business school? Is it realistic to expect that a
series of simulations and cleverly designed case studies can equip a
student with the necessary qualities that he (or she) would need to
call upon several years after graduation?

The answer is that, in view of the relative youth and inexperience
of students in business schools, coupled with severe time constraints, there is no hope of constructing a programme to provide a
comprehensive coverage of all the attributes listed in the table. This
is why business schools tend to concentrate on three of the four

elements of the knowledge base, to devote a great deal of time to academic subjects related to them, and to allocate less time to personal skills, and even less to the art of managing.

The result is little emphasis on training and more on education, the premiss being that the most important thing that a young person needs to learn is how to think, to learn what questions to ask, and to learn how to weigh the evidence presented to him. Is it then surprising that business schools' curricula lean towards analysis of the tangible rather than speculation on the intangible, and that economics, social science, techniques and modelling tend to dominate?

All this helps to explain the reasons for the business schools' present dilemmas. It is not that they are not aware of the needs of business and industry, or that they belittle the importance of certain perceived attributes. Rather, it is a matter of trying to offer, within given constraints of time and resources, what the schools are currently best at doing for the *majority* of the student body. The aim is not to produce instant effective managers, but people who have a good understanding of the managerial scene and consequently would have a better chance of becoming effective managers one day. The business school is not a substitute for the thrilling experience of success and for the hard lessons of failure in real life. What the school *can* do is to undertake the most difficult but rewarding task of helping people to comprehend, and hopefully cope with, such eventualities.

The need for continuing education

The unrealistic expectations of critics of management education largely stem from their misconception that an MBA programme should prepare students for a lifetime career, as if going to a business school is equivalent to taking a pill that ensures immunity for life. What they must realize is that management education is a *continuing process*, of which the MBA is merely the first step. Good managers continue learning all the time, from new tasks and responsibilities, from colleagues and from competitors. The needs of managers vary enormously, since they are largely determined by their background and experience, and these needs can be met by managers going back to school at different times in their careers, for updating and upgrading their knowledge and expertise. Some employers recognize the desirability of spreading training and education over many years, and if such a scheme were to be more widely promulgated throughout the business world, the pressure on schools to provide it all at the MBA stage would be greatly relieved.

All this may sound as a long-winded apologia for business schools. It is not intended to be. It must be admitted that some school programmes have atrophied, that cases can be cited where narrow disciplines leave little room for imagination and creativity, that some lecturers pontificate about management theory and sophisticated paradigms without ever having set a foot on the shopfloor, that too much of the ensuing pretentious literature is totally divorced from reality. Furthermore, much of the empirical and anecdotal evidence presented in case studies is often unstructured and devoid of an analytical foundation, and the treatment of some subjects – such as business policy, which is discussed further in the next chapter – is unsuitable for the majority of MBA students.

To varying degrees, all these allegations are true and should not be brushed aside. They need to be investigated and properly explored, alongside the acknowledged strengths of the business schools, so that possible improvements and new orientations can be implemented. But the starting point must be a widespread acceptance by industry of the concept of continuing management education, with concomitant undertakings to collaborate with business schools in constructing long-term programmes for this purpose and sending staff to participate in them. It is only then that a true partnership between business and business schools would emerge to the benefit of all concerned.

Reference

Eilon, S. 1979. *Aspects of Management*, ch. 14. Oxford: Pergamon Press.

CHAPTER 18

Business policy for beginners

Tomorrow's captains of industry

It is axiomatic in the academic world that every self-respecting business school must have a business policy course as part of its curriculum. After all, graduates of business schools are expected to become tomorrow's captains of industry, and as such they would have to be fully adept at analysing overall corporate performance and be equipped to formulate policies for the future. It is only natural, then, for business school deans to conclude that their students should be adequately prepared for this exalted role, and what better way to achieve that aim than by teaching them business policy?

As indicated in the previous chapter, the whole ethos of business schools is based on the assumption that there exists a body of knowledge encompassing 'basic general principles of management' which can be taught to aspiring managers, irrespective of which business or industry they will be involved in. Similarly, it is argued that business policy can be taught, that it, too, has a body of knowledge and basic principles. The business of business schools is to enunciate these general principles and formalize theories with which all their students should be fully conversant. Armed with this invaluable knowledge, and with the skills needed to apply it, our future industrial leaders would then forge ahead to make their corporations more successful than ever before.

This so-called 'conceptual framework' seems to have been so universally accepted, that business policy has become one of the central compulsory courses that all business students have to take. In some MBA and MBA-look-alike programmes business policy has even become the core curriculum, the central 'integrative discipline', which aims to bring all the other taught courses together. The message to the students seems to be: 'This is what it is all about. The business policy case studies represent the kind of problems that you will encounter in industry when you leave this place. This is why business policy has been selected as the primary course in the programme and allocated the largest percentage of the available teaching time.'

This conceptual framework is invalid on two counts. First, it is necessary to question the implied premiss that the realm of business policy is indeed the one in which a young manager would be expected to operate soon after graduation, and secondly serious doubts need to be expressed about the way in which the subject is taught in the classroom.

Students' background

Examination of the background of students enrolled in the master's programme at many business schools reveals that they constitute a very mixed bag in terms of ability, experience and motivation. Most are in their early twenties without any industrial experience whatsoever, coming straight from a first University degree, in search of fame and fortune in the commercial or industrial world. A fairly large percentage come from developing countries, all convinced that an MBA from a British or American university would unlock doors to better things in life (some vaguely think of the MBA as a means of avoiding a return to their country of origin).

In addition, there are some who have had one or two years' experience in a lowly capacity in industry (engineers who have become disenchanted with the idea of following engineering careers, scientists who have become disillusioned with the prospects open to them as scientists in industry, arts graduates who have been thrust into mundane and boring jobs, seemingly without any prospects at all), who rightly perceive the MBA programme as a conversion course that would relabel them and make them more attractive to employers in the job market.

And finally, there is a small number of older students, who have had some personal experience of the satisfaction and frustration encountered in an industrial environment, who want to enrich their store of knowledge and know exactly what they came for. Unlike members of the former two groups, who have only a vague notion of what type of enterprise, or even industry, they wish to seek a career in, most of the older and experienced students have firm views about their future careers and many already have job offers from past employers or sponsors to look forward to.

Teaching many of the subjects in an MBA programme to such a heterogeneous group in one single class is almost impossible; teaching them business policy is a nonsense. Leaving aside the fact that many overseas students have to overcome a cultural shock of facing an environment very different from their own (even apart from possible language difficulties), the perceptions of what business is all about are so diverse for people who have not been exposed to industrial life, that throwing them 'into the deep end', so to speak, to face problems of decision making at the very top of the corporate hierarchy, is bound to leave many of them bewildered and bemused. Even if they do not drown, it should not be concluded that they have all benefited from the experience.

Misconceptions of the traditional business policy course

In the context of a learning process, it is easy to confuse superficial understanding with comprehension. The fact that a student understands the words of a statement delivered in a lecture or in the course of a discussion does not mean that he (or she) has fully comprehended its meaning and the profound relationships that it may imply. The fact that a student can use the latest buzzwords and impress his tutors and colleagues with spurious use of jargon, is no proof of genuine comprehension either. Knowledge in this area may be no more than skin deep, and a little knowledge, coupled with bravado, may well be dangerous.

This is not to argue, of course, that business policy should not be taught at all to students without industrial experience. There is clearly a need to give them *some* background, a kind of an introduction, without the pretension that it represents a solid theory, or a proven recipe of how to direct strategy at the top (whether the body of knowledge, in as far as it exists in this area, can amount to a 'theory' is another contentious issue, which was discussed briefly in the previous chapter).

What is argued here is against the proposition that business policy should constitute a dominant core of an MBA programme. The justification that a business policy course is naturally a focal point for integrating the whole business school programme is highly questionable. And the presumption that business policy case studies prepare students to become effective problem solvers and decision makers at the very top of an industrial organization is even more ludicrous. You can teach an athlete in the classroom all there is to know about running: the physics and chemistry of the body, the consumption of oxygen and nutrients, the strengths and weaknesses of the competition; you can show him all the tapes of great runners, past and present; you can conduct endless stimulations in a laboratory environment. But you would be foolish to expect him to become a champion on the track soon after leaving the classroom.

The danger of unrealistic expectations

To implant these expectations is not just naive, it is harmful. The danger is that students would actually believe the sales pitch, namely that a master's course of one or two years' duration can convert them from being nobodies to becoming super-professionals. And evidently, many do believe that, as implied in their immediate expectations of very high salaries and rapid advancement prospects.

Not for them are the modest ranks of management, even as a means of gaining experience. Many think that they don't need experience. They believe they can go straight to the top and that they can do as good a job as those who are already at the top. After all, they have been exposed to all these case studies, which encapsulate many years of industrial know-how. And they have been *told* that they can do it. Many have even been coached to state at job interviews that their aim is indeed to get to the top, as quickly as possible, waiting just long enough to allow the current incumbents to vacate their chairs.

For a small percentage of aspirants this gambit does work and they are indeed a success story. They are courted by aggressive financial corporations and consulting firms (is it not amazing how many such firms recruit inexperienced MBAs to become corporate and strategy consultants?), they get paid extremely well and are rapidly promoted. But there are many more instances of MBAs becoming frustrated by the lack of career progression in line with their aspirations, only to be matched by the employers' bewilderment at the unrealistic expectations of the new recruits. Perhaps it is appropriate to ask whether the relatively few success stories, which are often hyped for promotional purposes, do not hide the real disappointments widely felt in the MBA market-place.

There is clearly room for more research on the non-success stories, as seen by the MBAs who have not 'made it' to the boardroom level, and as seen by many disenchanted employers. The point to stress here is that the *primary* role of business schools should not be to groom young MBAs for the top jobs, but to prepare them to become effective managers at the lower levels in the hierarchy, certainly for several years after graduation, until their performance can justify more exalted aspirations. This would be a much more realistic mission for business schools and would help to keep unwarranted expectations under control.

Teaching business policy

My other reservation about business policy courses stems from the *method of teaching*. In spite of the claim that there is a solid body of knowledge in this field, and in spite of a large number of books and journals which continue to proliferate (business policy and strategy has become probably one of the fastest growing areas in publishing), teaching business policy in most business schools relies heavily, if not exclusively, on case studies.

Business cases are often likened to those in the fields of law and medicine, where they aim to record and encapsulate past experience, thereby helping the student and practitioner to navigate through uncharted waters. If a problem occurs for which there are close enough precedents, then the experience of those who have handled such precedents, armed with the knowledge of subsequent events, can provide a reliable guide as to what courses of action can be contemplated and which are likely to bring about a satisfactory outcome.

It is, therefore, claimed that as the student cannot be exposed to real situations during the course of his (or her) studies, case studies provide the essence of simulated experience. This is why many schools insist that as many cases be presented as possible, so that the student can encounter a wide variety of problems and enterprises, and thereby add to his fund of knowledge on the subject. The more cases the student covers, so the argument goes, the better equipped he would be when the time comes to act in real life.

The shortcomings of case studies

There is nothing wrong, in principle, with this notion, except its naivety. Even if we assume that the student's ability as a problem solver and skill as a decision maker increase with the number of case studies covered in the classroom (and this is indeed a big assumption), the quality of the cases must surely play an important part in the learning process. Most of the business case studies encountered in business schools are lamentably poor.

They often consist of a hotchpotch of bits of information of inexorable superficiality, peppered with newspaper reports, truncated interviews and thoroughly unreliable journalistic commentaries. All this is said to require the student to check for consistency and to piece together a coherent story of the enterprise under scrutiny. But the picture presented in the case study is always incomplete, and vital information is often missing or subject to bias. This, it is said, represents reality. 'This is what it's like out there. You rarely enjoy the luxury of being able to ask for more information, or to afford the time and money needed to get it. So, this is what you have in this case. Do your best with it.'

It sounds like a convincing argument, but it can (and does) encourage superficial treatment. It is so easy for the student (and for the tutor for that matter) to make unwarranted assumptions, to come up with 'new' information gleaned from undisclosed or dubious sources, and to give more or less credence to selective data enumerated in the case, and thereby destroy the analytical process needed to weigh the pros and cons of alternative strategies. Some cases almost descend to the formula of a Perry Mason episode, where a crucial piece of evidence is withheld until the very last moment and suddenly sprung on the jury with the effect of overturning what would have been an obvious verdict up to that point.

The dramatic effect may be spectacular, but whether the student's analytical faculties are thereby sharpened is another matter. At the end of the day, irrespective of how meticulous and detailed the written case material is, it is bound to contain many value judgements and to involve imponderables, and this is not something that an inexperienced student can fully appreciate and learn from.

How business policy should fit into the programme

So, what is the answer? If a business policy course is to be included in the programme, how should it be structured in order to avoid all these drawbacks? I take the liberty of relating my own experience of teaching this subject, and suggest the following framework.

First, let us start with the proposition that not all business school graduates will be involved with the analysis and formulation of corporate policies and strategies, at least for several years after joining their corporations. It follows, therefore, that an *introductory course* on business policy, compulsory to all students, would suffice, but that it should not dominate the programme.

Indeed, its importance should be regarded on a par with other subjects, such as economics, statistics, finance and organization behaviour. In view of the unsatisfactory nature of more available case studies, the course should concentrate on basic concepts, on criteria for evaluating corporate performance, on the measurement process, on the importance of the contributions made by various managerial functions to the overall wellbeing of the enterprise, and on the likely interactions between them. As in other courses, many examples can be cited to demonstrate specific arguments, but the use of full-fledged case studies (if any) should be subservient to the presentation of the 'conceptual framework', rather than dominate it. There are numerous well-written textbooks (with little or even no case material) that can amply serve the purpose.

Many introductory subjects are offered in an MBA programme in order to ensure that the individual student is sufficiently conversant with the roles and responsibilities of various functions in the business. But during the later part of the programme, the student can opt to specialize in certain areas, such as finance, operations management, personnel, and so on. A similar opportunity should be given to those wishing to extend their study of business policy and strategy. Many of the students opting for this course would be older than the average, and perhaps they should be required to have had industrial and preferably managerial experience as a prerequisite.

A personal experience

A colleague and I have run such an *elective* course (for further details see Betts (1978)). It consisted of two parts. The first took the form of a series of lectures, elaborating on basic relevant concepts introduced elsewhere in the programme, and this was supplemented by a suitable reading list, which students were expected to cover. The second part consisted of case studies, but these were not selected from textbooks; *they were live cases, written by the students themselves*.

A group of students (usually six to eight) was assigned a real enterprise to study and given 2–6 months to write a report. Their brief was: 'Your team has been asked by the CEO of company X to analyse the performance and strategy of the company and to submit a report with your recommendations for future action'; alternatively, 'Your team has been asked by the CEO of company Y to analyse the performance and current and future strategies of company X and to submit a report with your findings and conclusions'. (The alternative brief meant that the students could not assume that the reader of the report would necessarily be familiar with the background history of company X or its operations.) It was up to the team to determine what information to gather and where to get it from, who to interview, how to divide the work among members of the team, and how to write and present their report, which had to be submitted by a prescribed deadline.

The report was circulated to the other members of the class (i.e. to those who were not authors of the report but belonged to other teams, writing reports on other companies). They were required to study the contents of the report and formulate questions for discussion in class. In addition, those who were not authors of the report had each to complete a brief written assignment with his (or her) views of the most important issues facing the board of directors (issues, not solutions!) of the company in question.

At a subsequent seminar for the whole class the authors of the report made a brief oral presentation, highlighting certain problems raised in their report and filling in further background, as necessary. Usually, each author was encouraged to make an individual presentation on his (or her) contribution to the report. The proceedings were presided over by a student, chosen by the team to act as editor/chairman for the occasion. There then followed a question and answer session and a discussion of the main issues raised, aided and abetted by the two faculty members present.

Copies of the report were sent to the chairman or CEO of the company (who had, of course, been contacted several months earlier and agreed to take part in the exercise), and a week or two after the presentation seminar a second seminar took place, at which the chairman or CEO or sometimes both were present, often accompanied by another director or senior executive. I took the chair at these sessions, starting with a brief introduction and with an undertaking that the whole proceedings would be treated as strictly confidential.

The visitor then gave his reactions to the report, corrected mistakes and misconceptions, amplified on the background that had led to past key policy decisions, and gave his views on the conclusions and recommendations. Then followed a lively discussion, in which all the students (and not just the authors of the report) were encouraged to take part. The session, which was held in the late afternoon, culminated with a formal dinner party, at which the visitors, the authors and the two faculty members could enjoy further informative and interesting discussions in a relaxed atmosphere.

Concluding remarks

This is not a formula that would suit every business school. For one thing, our seminar could not have been effectively conducted for a very large class, and we felt that limiting its size to about 40 students (covering six to seven companies) was as much as we could undertake in each academic year. Furthermore, I cannot pretend that running a business policy course on these lines was anything but hard work for the students, and even more so for the tutors, for whom the amount of preparatory work was far in excess of a normal course which follows a set textbook. Apart from guiding students in the pursuit of their investigations and during the report-writing stage, there was a fair amount of briefing required before the consent of CEOs could be secured to proceed with the studies of their companies.

Business schools with hundreds of enrolled students may reasonably conclude that they would not be justified in allocating resources to run a business policy course in this way, particularly when the number of students opting for it is likely to be large. What, then, is the alternative? I would argue that, in essence, the framework outlined above is valid for larger classes too, except that it may be necessary to dispense with the live participation of some or all the CEOs. The benefits of the course would consequently be greatly diminished, but even in a truncated form it would be superior to the use of conventional case studies taken from textbooks. In addition, a series of seminars on the lines indicated above would be very appropriate for post-MBAs in their thirties, when the experience of active participation in writing the case reports and in subsequent discussions could be invaluable.

Looking back at our business policy seminar (which, over a period of 20 years, covered well over 120 enterprises), I believe that they were a great success. The fact that they involved chairmen and CEOs served as an important focal point for students opting for this course. It gave them a rare opportunity to meet people responsible for making key policy decisions, and to discuss real (and not hypothetical) strategies. It taught them how and where to look for information, how to assemble and analyse facts, how to work as a team, how to present a report both in written form and orally. But perhaps more than anything, the business policy seminar helped them to appreciate what is, after all, the ultimate aim of an educational process, namely to think and to be able to formulate good questions.

References

Betts, R. J. 1978. The teaching of business policy – a fresh approach. *Omega* 6 (6), 515–22.

Index

accountability 19, 36, 42, 134–48, 150, 162, 176, 182, 192
accounting 74, 184
aerospace 79, 80
allocation methods 114–24, 127–9, 134–48
ambiguity 12, 15, 51–2, 164
analysis 3, 4, 9, 26, 57, 60, 63, 115, 132, 153, 192
appraisal schemes 156
arm's length 139
arrogance 203
art of managing 194
asset turn 91–8, 101
association – *see* cause and effect
authority – *see* accountability

banking 85, 142, 168, 173, 179
'banking' 177
bankruptcy 41 (*see also* corporate failure)
behaviour 1, 2, 48–9, 73, 186
Bell, J. 75, 82
benefits in kind 168
Betts, J. R. 207, 210
board functions 42
board size 39–47
bottom line 71–82
budget 60, 61, 63, 66, 136, 169
building materials 79
bureaucracy xiv, 161, 182, 184, 187
business policy 15, 200–10
business school xv, 28, 80, 184, 188, 189, 190–9, 192, 195–210
buzzwords 202

carob tree 82
case studies 26, 27, 32, 36–8, 125–33, 172–4, 203–5
cash flow – *see* DCF
causality – *see* cause and effect
cause and effect 2, 45–7, 104, 122
centralization 19, 35
CEO (Chief Executive Officer) xii, 15–24, 40, 43, 47, 49–51, 58, 60–1, 76, 177, 207–9
Chaganti, R.S. 39–47
Channel Tunnel 79
chaos 1, 2, 48 (*see also* volatility)

China 72
choice 2–4, 131
City 74
common misery 63
competition 16, 33, 54, 69, 72, 177, 186, 192
computer industry 185
computer(s) 5, 7, 8, 35, 78, 141–3, 145, 177
Concorde 79
Conference Board 42, 47
conflict xiii, 63, 125–33, 172–5
constraints 1, 3, 52, 64, 69, 70, 133, 134, 195
construction 56, 69, 79
continuing education 198–9
control 16, 25, 47, 65, 84, 114, 144–5, 146, 148, 150, 156, 163–4
corporate failure 39–47
corporate objectives – *see* objectives
corporate performance xi, xiii, 12, 18–39, 41, 46, 54, 60, 72–3, 83–104, 113, 125, 163
corporate planning 17, 81, 108, 144
corporate success – *see* success
corporate survival 41
cost centre 60, 136, 143
cost cutting – *see* cost(s)
cost(s) xiv, 12, 28, 30, 36, 53, 60–3, 65–9, 76–7, 87, 100, 101, 110, 112, 115–23, 129, 131, 135–41, 143–5
cost-benefit analysis 63, 76–8, 80
cost-plus 67, 68
creativity 183, 194, 197
credit rating xi, 74
crime detection 78
criteria xiv, 1, 3, 4, 11–12, 26, 38, 84, 89–104, 111–13, 114, 123
customer service 173–5
customers 20, 22, 26, 29, 140, 173, 195

DCF (discounted cash flow) 75–81
decentralization – *see* centralization
decision categories 5, 7, 8, 10
decision making xiv, 2–13, 40, 48, 51, 55, 56, 58, 149, 157, 170
decision nodes 54–5
decision process – *see* decision making
decision variable 64
defence contracts 68

Index

design 3, 74, 144, 187, 192
determinants 25–39, 47
deterministic 10, 11
diagnosis – *see* analysis
disorder – *see* chaos
diversification 10
divide and rule 36, 70, 134–48
domestic appliances 172
dominance 96
Drucker, P. 153, 161
DSS (Decision Support Systems) 8, 14
duality syndrome 35

economies of scale 30, 31 (*see also* size)
efficiency 62, 72, 106, 107, 112, 128, 146, 170
Eilon, S. 14, 24, 59, 104, 113, 148, 161, 189, 199
employee of the week 169
employees xii, 19, 21–3, 26, 30, 62, 105, 154–5, 168, 169–70, 175–6, 187, 195
engineering 17
eps (earnings per share) 18, 19
evolution v. revolution 55
expectations 191–2, 203
experience xv, 9, 202
experimentation 27
exploitation 71

facilitators 175
fast buck 80
feedback 3, 16, 157, 159, 164
financial measures 20, 26, 69, 90–104
fire-fighting 61
'first class men' 154
forecasting 186
freedom of action (or choice) 1, 4, 35
French, S. 76, 82
frequency 6–8, 10

games 10, 11
Germany 75, 81, 191
given 12, 64, 66–9, 115
goals – *see* objectives
Gold, B. 106, 109, 110, 113
great man theory 28

head-office functions 144–6
heuristics 8
hidden agenda 51
hierarchy of needs 154
hospitals 112
hotels 36
Hungary 72

ICL 130

incentive schemes 165–7, 180 (*see also* rewards)
incentives – *see* rewards
income tax 168
information 3, 4, 10, 11, 42, 54–5, 123, 131, 142, 161
innovation xii, 22, 31, 32, 49
Institutional Fund Managers Association 75, 82
inter-firm comparison 106
inventory 10, 111, 143
investment appraisal 10, 12
investment banks – *see* merchant banks
IRR (internal rate of return) 76
IT (information technology) 142

jam tomorrow 166, 168
Japan 75, 81, 191
job description 157–8, 163–4
job design 163–4
job enlargement 154
John Lewis 170
Johnson, L. B. 189

labour productivity 106, 110
lateral thinking 183, 186–7
layout 10, 11
leadership 184, 194, 196–7
learning 14, 177
Leavitt, H. 183, 184, 185, 186, 188, 189
LP (linear programming) 10, 184

M25 78
Mali, P. 106, 108, 110, 111, 113
management attributes 193–4
management consultants xiv, xv, 14, 15, 22, 24, 26, 37, 58, 60, 114, 136, 151, 161, 187
management development – *see* training
management philosophy xiv, 25–31, 68, 70, 134, 136, 146, 154, 188, 190, 199
management school – *see* business school
management science 133 (*see also* OR)
management services 35, 140–2
management, theory of – *see* management philosophy
managerial echelons – *see* managerial hierarchy
managerial functions 194, 196
managerial hierarchy xii, 7, 17, 24, 36, 70, 84, 183
managerial process 70, 162
managerial style xiii, 47
managerial traits 157–8
manpower planning 157, 160
market dominance 29, 31
market research 64

market, market share xii, 16, 29, 31, 49, 67, 126–7, 131, 137–41, 192
market-oriented approach 69
Marsh, P. 75, 82
Maslow, A. H. 154–5, 161
Maslowism – *see* Maslow
MBO (management by objectives) 106, 109
MCDM (multi-criteria decision making) 83, 84
McGregor, D. 151–2, 154–6, 161
measurement xiv, 3, 4, 33–4, 54, 56, 111–12, 114, 164, 196
merchant banking 85–7, 178
mining 78
Mintzberg, H. 9, 12, 14
MIS (management information system) 142, 145
misconceptions 202
mission xiv, 15–24
modelling, models xiv, 3–5, 10–11, 33, 56–7, 114, 184, 196, 198
monitoring 4, 16, 25, 42, 114, 163, 164, 196
motivation 154, 183, 201 (*see also* rewards)
multi-criteria xiii, 52, 83, 84, 88, 89
multi-products 115–20, 137

non-executive directors 40, 43, 44, 45
non-programmed decisions 5–12, 184
NPV (net present value) 76, 78, 79

O&M 60
objectives xii, xiii, 3, 4, 10, 11, 15–20, 42, 47, 51–3, 55–6, 114–15, 133, 135, 153, 156–7, 159, 162–3, 173
Ofstad, H. 4, 14
Omega xvi
operating profit 99
opportunistic approach 68
optimizing 37, 52–3, 57, 68
OR (Operational Research) 5, 9, 48–59, 141–2, 175, 184
organization chart 134–5
organization hierarchy – *see* organization
organization structure factor 30
organization xiii, xiv, 10, 15, 17, 30–1, 33, 36–7, 134–7, 142, 146, 149, 150, 162, 164, 176, 185–7, 195
organizational change 176
overheads 114–24, 127–9
ownership 23, 170

P/E (profit-to-earnings ratio) 73
Pareto curve 34
pathfinding 183–6
penalties 166, 178–9
performance appraisal 149–61

performance criteria – *see* criteria, corporate performance
performance measures – *see* criteria, corporate performance
Perry Mason 206
personal traits 156–8
Peter's principle 170
pharmaceuticals 75, 80
physical laws – *see* science
piece rate 177, 179–80
policy 163 (*see also* mission, objectives)
prediction 3, 8
problem solving 5, 8, 9, 13, 184–5, 196, 203
procurement – *see* purchasing
product dominance 29, 31, 32
production control 143
productivity factor 29
productivity xiv, 29, 31, 32, 72, 105–13, 172
profit 65–9, 71–5, 85, 87, 88, 89, 93–5, 99, 102, 115–23, 135
profit centre 60, 63, 136–8
profit margin 66, 67–8, 73, 91–103, 116, 118–21
profit sharing 130
programmed decisions 5–14
purchasing 35, 143, 145, 172

quality 20, 175
quarrying 79
queuing models 10
quick fix 64

R&D (research and development) 22, 29, 34, 53–4, 80–1, 144–6, 151, 171, 175, 179, 182 (*see also* innovation)
ratios – *see* corporate performance, criteria
recruitment xii, 36, 62, 111, 149, 164, 183, 187, 191
relative changes 97
remuneration – *see* rewards
replication 6–10
research 15, 39–47, 49, 83, 112, 181–2
research methodology 43–6
resource allocation 16, 31–2, 87, 107, 134–5, 150, 196
responsibility – *see* accountability
revenue 65–8, 76, 86–7, 92–4, 96, 101–2, 115–23, 128–9, 135, 140
rewards systems – *see* rewards
rewards xi, 21, 23, 26, 30, 129, 130, 132, 135, 160, 162–80
Richard III 81
risk 10–12, 56, 80, 135, 181–2
risk aversion 11, 56, 80
ROCE (return on capital) 18, 19, 52, 73, 90–9, 101, 103

Index

ROE (return on equity) 85–8
routine decisions 5–10
routine tasks 164

sales 64, 66, 92, 127, 136–7, 173–4
sales commission 173, 177
satisficing 52–3
scheduling problems 10, 11
science 2, 48–9, 188
scientific method – *see* science, OR
self actualization 154, 155
senior executives xiii, 15, 23, 25, 42, 49, 150
Shakespeare 81
shareholders 19, 22, 26, 42, 74, 85, 195
short-term xi, xiii, 52–3, 61, 64, 73, 74, 75, 82, 115
short-termism 76, 80, 81, 82
Simon, A. H. 2, 5, 8, 14, 53
size xii, 30, 33 (*see also* economies of scale)
skill 6, 21, 63, 196–7, 200
social responsibility 42
social science 194, 198
Soviet Union 72
spare parts 173
Special Committee of the House of Representatives 155
stick and carrot xi, 165
stock options 168
stop-go 62
strategic decisions – *see* strategy
strategy xii, 13, 17, 23, 31, 53–9, 70, 81
structure 1–15, 39, 163
success xi–xiii, 18, 25–6, 41
symphony orchestra 163

take-over xii, 54, 74

targets – *see* objectives
Taylor, F. W. 154, 155, 161
Taylorism – *see* Taylor
technology 28–31, 49, 54–5, 113, 184, 194
telecommunications 75
Thames Barrier 79
theories – *see* management philosophies
theory and practice xiv, xv, 48
think tank 48, 50
threats 55
trade-offs xiii, 51, 83, 84
training xii, 8, 30, 62, 63, 73, 145, 150, 157, 160, 164
transfer pricing 125–33, 137–48
travel time 77–8
treasury 35
TSP (Travelling salesman problem) 10, 11

UK 71, 73, 75, 169, 191, 192
uncertainty 10–15, 164, 181
USA 41, 71, 73, 75, 169, 184, 190, 191, 192

vehicle fleet 173
vision 16, 23, 24, 184
volatility 2, 49

Wall Street 74
Wilmot, R. 130
Wilson, W. B. 155
work study 177
workforce – *see* employees
working practices 176
World War 50

Yugoslavia 72